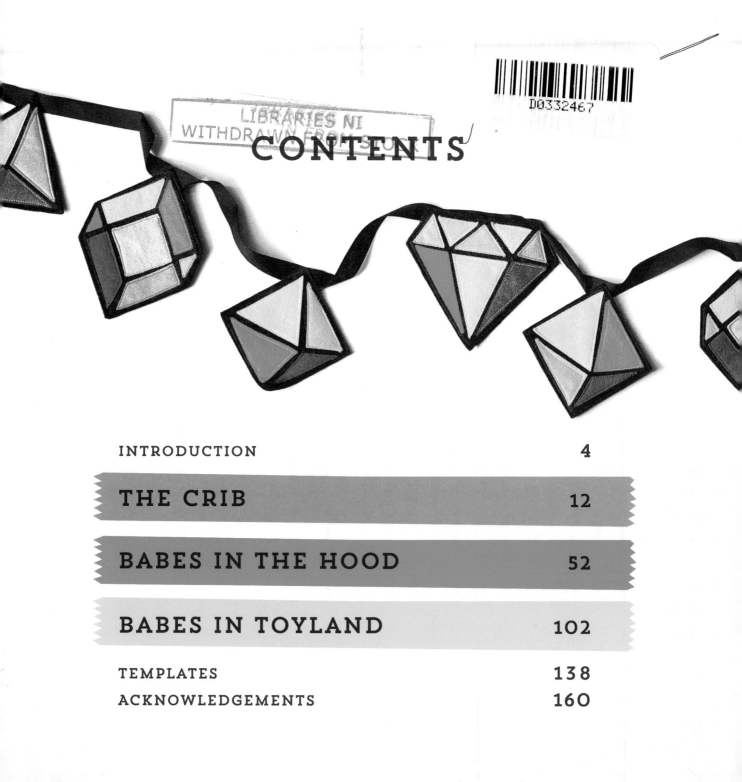

CONTENTS

FROM THE CRADLE TO THE CRAFT TABLE

The bumpy ride to motherhood is full of all sorts of exciting, and sometimes even daunting, new challenges and adventures. For me, it was a whirlwind of excitement, anticipation and what seemed like masses of planning and preparation! One of the most angst-inducing aspects of kitting yourself out for the new arrival can be the potential cost, as every new mum to be will have a long list of essentials to acquire.

Getting ready for my own daughter to arrive brought with it as many practical questions as it did style decisions. Having a baby is such a personal and intimate experience it seems only fitting that the objects collected to feather their nest should reflect the personality, taste and style of the new parents. As a creative mama, I was utterly unimpressed with what was available on the high street, where buying into generic baby brands seemed totally contrary to my creative inclinations. I did, however, soon discover a wonderful world of stylish and exciting independent designers, whose baby clothing and accessories although lovely cost more than I wanted to spend on something that would, in reality, last only a couple of months. Babies grow out of clothes and toys so quickly – almost from month to month – so I thought it would be so much more satisfying, not to mention kinder on the pockets, to get busy and create my own custom-made baby gear instead. And I soon realised how much fun making things for babies could be! Most items are small and simple enough to sew in just a short time – ideal for keeping busy until the baby arrives – as well as providing some relaxing downtime activity between naps once your baby is born.

Almost all the projects in this book were designed within the first year of my daughter's life and include my must-haves for living stylishly alongside your baby. Better yet, the unique and useful items are completely customisable, so can be crafted to suit the parents' personal style. You will find instructions for a selection of nursery decorations, baby accessories, clothes, toys and gifts all organised into three nifty chapters.

THE CRIB caters for all your nursery needs; I will show you how to patchwork a cute and contemporary chevron baby quilt or make some modern mobiles from leftover felt scraps from your fabric stash.

BABES IN THE HOOD shows you how to create your own on-the-go accessories, essential for taking your baby out and about, such as DIY dummy clips, plus how to pimp your pram with a customised buggy blanket or pram toys.

BABES IN TOYLAND will give you loads of ideas and inspiration for inventing toys to stimulate your baby and help them to explore their developing senses with a selection of handmade playthings, including soft toys, flash cards, building blocks and stacking rings.

All the projects make excellent gifts, so whether you're an expectant mum eagerly anticipating your baby's arrival, or a friend, relative or even a dad-to-be looking to stitch a thoughtful handmade gift to welcome a new arrival, this book will provide endless ideas and inspiration. Perfect for those nesting on a budget or those who just want to assert their own style, projects are accessible to both the beginner and the seasoned seamstress alike, with plenty of items at a range of skill levels, all designed with style-savvy parents and tiny trendsetters in mind.

TIPS

GETTING READY TO SEW

Before you start stitching there are just a few basic sewing tools you'll need to gather as well as some simple sewing techniques and tricks to master.

BASIC TOOLKIT

1. Hand-sewing needles

2. Sewing machine and needles plus ball-point needle for sewing knits and stretch

3. An assortment of coloured sewing threads

4. Fabric scissors and paper scissors

5. Pins and safety pins

6. Tape measure

7. Ruler

8. Fabric marker pen or tailor's chalk

9. Rotary cutter, mat and quilting grid for patchwork (handy but not essential!)

10. Iron and ironing board

11. Turning tool – like a blunt pencil or knitting needle for poking out sharp corners.

MATERIALS

FABRICS

When selecting fabrics for sewing your handmade baby items and clothing, I suggest choosing natural, breathable fabrics such as cotton, linen or wool blends – generally anything that is to be worn against babies' skin should be soft, comfortable and baby-safe. Quilting-weight cottons, felt, fleece or cuddle-soft plushie fabrics are fun to work with and make great choices for stitching baby toys or non-wearable accessories. Another consideration when selecting fabrics is to keep in mind the overall use of the finished item and whether or not it will need to be washed, as this will effect the durability of the fabrics you should use. All projects have suggested fabrics listed in the materials section.

POLYESTER FIBERFILL

Polyester fiberfill is used for stuffing toys or as filling for cushions and can be found sold in pre-packaged bags priced by weight from most good craft stores or haberdasheries. A typical bag usually weighs 250g.

WADDING

Wadding is used as a filling to sit between two layers of fabric to add extra warmth, body and texture to quilts and other items that require additional padding. It can be found sold by the metre at craft shops, fabric stores and good haberdasheries in a variety of different weights and thicknesses. Natural cotton wadding is recommended for baby blankets, quilts or clothing. Polyester wadding is an economical choice for all other items. For beginners it is best to choose a fairly thin wadding, which will be easier to sew through the machine.

INTERLINING

Interlining is a stabiliser used to add extra strength and stability between layers of fabric. It can be bought in different weights and thicknesses, either in a sew-in or fusible form. Fusible webbing is used for bonding fabrics together and invaluable for preparing and stitching appliqué. Bonda-web and HeatnBond Lite are both good brands.

TRICKS

PRE-SHRINKING FABRICS

Before preparing and cutting out fabric for your sewing projects, make sure you wash, dry and press all fabrics to prevent your finished hand-sewn treasures from distorting when eventually laundered. This is called pre-shrinking.

PRESSING

Always press fabric before cutting out and pinning on your pattern. As a tip always press from the wrong side of the fabric and against the grain lines. Press your projects with a hot steam iron but remember, do not distort the fabric by ironing back and forth. Press finished seams either open flat or to one side.

CUTTING

Before measuring and marking out your fabric, you need to line your patterns or templates up against the straight lengthwise grain of the fabric. The selvedge (the non-frayed bound woven edge of the fabric) runs parallel to the lengthwise grain, so use that as your guide and place the patterns or templates parallel to this edge before cutting out. Some patterns require cutting against the crosswise grain – follow cutting out instructions at the beginning of each project. Always lay fabric out flat when measuring and marking out to make sure you cut accurately – a flat cutting surface and some good lighting will make all the difference.

PATTERNS AND TEMPLATES

All templates and patterns needed for projects are provided. Simply size up and trace out onto paper before cutting out with a pair of paper scissors.

NOTCHES

Some patterns will have notch markings on them to help with joining and matching pattern seams. Clip these approx. 4–6mm into the seam allowance.

WORKING WITH PATTERNS

SORT THE PATTERN

Before staring a project, take some time to look at your pattern pieces and familiarise yourself with the instructions and seam positioning to prevent any mistakes that may occur in the cutting out stage.

FOLD THE FABRIC

Often a pattern will ask you to cut out against the fold of the fabric – simply fold the fabric as directed in the pattern instructions and lay the pattern piece with the fold line against the straight grain fold of the fabric.

LAYOUT THE PATTERN

Laying out the pattern is one of the most important parts of the sewing process as it helps lay the foundations for easy sewing. Before measuring and cutting out you will have to make sure the pattern is lined up against the straight grain of the fabric. Use the selvedge (the non-frayed bound edge of the fabric) that runs parallel to the lengthwise grain as your guide. The cross grain, which is the diagonal grain of the fabric known as the bias is used for cutting out patterns that require some give or stretch.

Before pinning your pattern, make sure you have a large enough flat surface to cut out. If you are working with very large pieces of fabric, such as when making a quilt, and you don't have a large enough table, then you may want to use the floor. Lay your patterns out onto the wrong side of your fabric, taking layout directions from the pattern and template instructions. If you are cutting patterns out against the fold on double thickness fabric, then lay your patterns onto the wrong side of the fabric. If you are cutting from single thickness than cut out on the right side of the fabric.

PINNING

Always pin fabric together against the seam lines at a perpendicular angle with pinheads facing to the right. This makes removing pins as you sew much easier and swifter. Place pins approx. 7.5–10cm apart and mark out the corner seam allowances as this will help you to gauge where to pivot when sewing corner seams on the machine.

SEAM ALLOWANCES

Always check seam allowance guidelines at the beginning of each project. Trim off extra seam allowances to approx. 4–6mm to reduce extra bulk in seams. Clip corners to ensure sharp points and clip and notch curved seams – see below.

CURVED SEAMS EXPLAINED

Curved seams must be either clipped or notched before turning right sided out, to help prevent bulky seams with excess fabric in the seam allowance.

The rule is:

Clip the seam allowance of outer curves
Notch the seam allowance of inner curves

TECHNIQUES

STITCHES

BABY SAFE

To ensure all your handmade items are baby-safe always use a strong, high-quality thread and take extra care to secure all your sewing notions and decorative finishes such as hook and loop fastening, poppers, trims and all stitching on seams or appliqué as securely as possible as babies will put anything and everything in their mouths as they explore the world around them. Likewise keep anything with loops or hanging strings and ties as short as possible. Hang handmade mobiles or crib garlands at a safe distance from your baby so they can see them but are not able to pull them down.

HAND-SEWING STITCHES

Almost all stitches are made from right to left and you should always fasten off and secure thread at the end of sewing with a couple of fix stitches made to the back of the fabric.

FIX STITCH

A fix stitch is literally just two or three stitches made on top of each other at the back of the fabric to secure thread in place before and after sewing.

STRAIGHT STITCH

A straight stitch should create a neat line of sturdy stitches with no gaps and is primarily used for joining seams. Insert the needle from the back of the fabric to the front then, in one movement, insert it back down 3mm along from where you just came up and back up again another 3mm along. Now insert the needle back down against the top of the stitch you just made and in one movement insert the needle up from the top of the furthest stitch. Repeat this movement to create one continuous line of overlapping stitches.

WHIPSTITCH

A nifty little stitch worked on top of the fabric to join two pieces together – ideal for working appliqué. Line up two pieces of fabric, then insert your needle from the back to the front of one piece. Now make a series of very small slanted stitches over the top edge of the two fabrics approx. 2mm apart.

SLIPSTITCH

This stitch is cleverly invisible from the right side of the fabric, which makes it perfect for hemming. It can also be used for anything that may be difficult to stitch on the machine, like attaching trims or finishing mitred corners or binding. Insert your needle from the back to the front of the fold of your hem to hide the knot, then make a series of stitches by picking up just one or two fibres from the fabric, then inserting the needle back through the folded edge approx. 6mm away (or more for bulkier fabrics) at a diagonal.

BLANKET STITCH

Blanket stitch is both functional as well as decorative. Typically used for tidying up raw edges (usually around blankets), it can also be used for stitching down appliqué and fixing fasteners like snaps and hooks and eyes. Blanket stitch is made from left to right rather than from right to left, and requires careful sewing to create a neat line. Insert the needle from the back of the fabric to the front, approx. 6mm from the edge. Then insert the needle back down just to the right of where you came up. Now, before pulling the thread tight, insert your needle through the loop. Pull the thread carefully and the stitch will

move up to sit along the top edge of the fabric. Continue inserting the needle from front to back and picking up the loop to create a line of linked stitches along the edge of your fabric.

MACHINE STITCHING

Here are a few basic machine stitches you will need to use for sewing your own handmade baby items.

STRAIGHT STITCH

This is the most basic machine stitch. Use different lengths of stitches for different types of fabric as directed in your owner's manual. You can use your stitch length dial to alter the length.

ZIGZAG STITCH

Zigzag stitching is great for finishing off open raw edges on appliqué or for finishing off inside hems to prevent fraying. Select the zigzag stitch on your machine and alter the width and the length of the zigzag to make the stitch size smaller or larger.

TOPSTITCHING

Topstitching is a straight stitch used for finishing hems and edges as it creates a firm, stable edge as well as keeps layers of fabric together. Always press and pin your hems to make stitching easier. Then sew as close to the folded seam edge as possible.

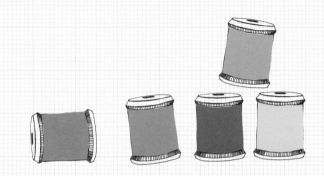

BINDING

Bindings are a neat and nifty way to decorate and finish off raw edges. They can be bought either ready-made or you can make your own from almost any material. Bias binding is binding cut on the bias (the fabric's stretchiest point) and is used especially for edging curves. Binding tape is cut on the straight of the grain and is great for attaching to straight edges. You can either bind by hand or for a quicker finish you can use the sewing machine.

Before you begin, ensure the work is properly squared off and to the correct size, with all corners at perfect right angles. Always start pinning your binding in the middle of one of the sides of your fabric rather than at a corner, as this will create a more seamless effect.

Double-fold bias binding will have a shorter fold and a longer fold. Open it out and place the shorter fold lined up against the raw edge of the back of your fabric. Stitch into place along the creased fold line using a straight stitch either on the machine or by hand. When you get to a corner, stop stitching approx. 6mm in from the edge, then fold the binding up to a 45-degree angle to create a neat fold at the corner, and continue stitching 6mm in from the edge as before. Continue folding and stitching the corners as described above until all sides are bound. Once you finish binding all sides and get back to the beginning where the two short ends meet, fold in the raw edge of the binding and stitch into place overlapping the unfolded binding to encase and finish.

To secure binding to the top of the fabric, fold the binding over the raw edge onto the right side of the fabric, pin into place and secure using hand-sewn slipstitches or stitch on the machine sewing as close to the folded edge as possible.

MITRING CORNERS

When you come to turning corners either with hems, edging or binding, you will find you have excess fabric that will need to be straightened and neatened to create a clean finish. This is known as mitring corners. If you are using a double-fold binding tape, encase the raw edges within the centre of the binding and pin in place along one side. Start stitching along the inner edge of the binding using a topstitch on the machine, making sure you catch all three layers as you go. Stitch right to the edge, then remove the work from the machine. Fold the binding around the corner to form a neat 45-degree angle; pin the pleat in place. Return the work to the machine and continue stitching around the inner edge of the binding.

APPLIQUÉ

Appliqué is a technique used to create a fabric decoration or embellishment, where fabric shapes are cut out and stuck down onto a background fabric then secured with stitches. It can be sewn by hand using a variety of stitches or on the machine using a straight, zigzag or satin stitch. Fusible webbing is often used as a stabiliser between the two fabrics to secure the appliqué cut-outs in place before stitching. Always cut appliqué shapes to the exact size and shape using the templates provided. When stitching, work slowly on the appliqué, taking extra care to sew around curves, pivoting and lifting the presser foot of the sewing machine in order to change the position and direction of stitching.

QUILTING

Stitching a layer of wadding between two layers of fabric and sewing over the top of the fabric is known as quilting. Not only does this provide protective padding but it also adds warmth, body and texture to your work.

Before quilting a project make sure that you cut out the fabrics to be quilted larger than the pattern pieces required, as the action of quilting will shrink the fabric as it becomes thick and bulky once sewn. Before stitching on the machine, tack the fabric and wadding layers together first as the bulkiness of the fabric will cause it to shift as you sew. Use a contrasting thread and start tacking stitches from the centre out, alternating between stitching lengthwise, crosswise and diagonally.

Mark out quilting lines on the fabric with tailor's chalk or use a quilting foot and feed bar, which will help guide the stitching lines. To start quilting, loosen the tension on your sewing machine and set it to a long straight stitch. Start quilting at the centre and work your way out towards the edge (this will also help prevent fabric from bulking). Feed the fabric–wadding sandwich through the machine, stitching down either in diagonal or parallel lines. The most popular quilting designs are diagonal quilting, square quilting and channel quilting (made up from parallel rows of stitching) They're all super easy to sew, so experiment with what works best for each particular project.

MAKING FABRIC TIES

Narrow fabric ties can be useful in a multitude of different ways for projects when an item requires a fabric fastening or tie.

As a general rule, cut the fabric out to four times the finished width required. Cut the fabric to the required finished length plus an extra 0.5cm for seam allowance at either short end for turning under raw seam edges to neaten.

Fold the fabric strip in half lengthwise with wrong sides together and press. Unfold and bring both long sides back into the middle to meet at the crease, again wrong sides together, and press. Fold in each of the open short ends by 0.5cm to the wrong side of the fabric and press. Finally, fold the strip in half again lengthwise to create the fabric tie and press and pin into place. Use a straight stitch to sew as close to the folded edges as possible to finish. Repeat for as many fabric ties required.

SEWING SNAP FASTENERS

Snap fasteners help to hold fabrics together and are a good choice for children's clothing as they are easy to undo. Just take extra care to affix them into place with some strong thread and secure stitching and always make sure to double-check stitching between washes.

Snap fasteners come in two parts – a socket and a stud. The stud part of the snap fastener is usually sewn onto the inside of the overlap and the socket part of the snap is usually sewn to the underside of the overlap. You want to make sure when sewing snaps that your stitches are invisible from the right side of the fabric, so take up only a few fibres from the right side of the fabrics as you stitch over the edge of each hole of the snap components to secure.

SEWING HOOK AND LOOP FASTENINGS

Hook and loop fastening is another two-part fastener, which can be found sold by the metre from haberdashery shops. One side is soft and made up from lots of little loops and the other side is rough and made up of lots of little hooks. When the two parts of the tape are stuck together, the fastening is temporarily bonded. Both parts of the tape can be stitched onto fabric using either a secure hand stitch or on the machine with a small zigzag or straight stitch.

THE CRIB
AT HOME WITH BABY

Feather your baby's nest with a fun and creative collection of simple-to-sew handmade nursery keepsakes and home accessories that are as stylish as they are useful. And what better way to welcome a baby into the world than with some hand-crafted treasures for that truly unique, personalised touch. This chapter contains patterns for everything you need to make your baby feel cosy, from stitching your own crib accessories such as pattern-tastic quilt covers, bright and bold crib bumpers and cute cushions to crafting decorative design accessories like mobiles and crib garlands to take them way past the nursery and beyond! With DIY décor ideas that parents will delight in as much as little ones, these handmade additions are guaranteed to be remembered and treasured forever.

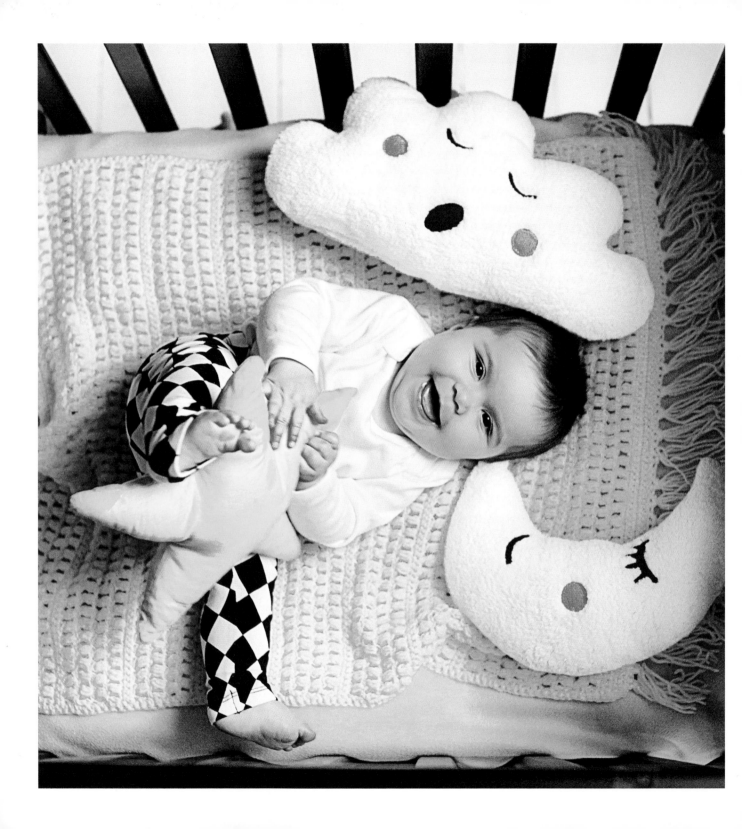

NURSERY CUSHIONS

Decorative cuddly cushions make adorable and snuggly soft additions to a baby's nursery and are my daughter's favourite of all my handmade creations so far. Make some up in luxe teddy-soft fabric or go playful with a selection of colourful cotton prints and patterns for a perfect pillow set including fluffy clouds, sleepy moons and bright stars. These cute cushions also double up as toys!

HOW TO CUT OUT THE TEMPLATES AND FABRICS

1. Using the cloud, star and moon templates on page 150 as a guide, draw them onto paper or thin card. Cut out the templates with paper scissors.

2. Mark out two of each shape on your chosen fabrics (one for the front, one for the back) and cut out.

3. Photocopy or trace the nursery cushion appliqué templates on page 150 onto paper or thin card. Cut out the templates with paper scissors. Mark and cut the appliqué details for the cushion faces as follows:

CLOUD
- 1 x cloud mouth
- 2 x cheek
- 2 x eye/mouth

MOON
- 1 x moon eye
- 1 x cheek
- 1 x eye/mouth

STAR
- 2 x star eye
- 1 x eye/mouth

continued on the next page

FINISHED SIZE
Cloud cushion – approx. 40 x 20cm
Moon cushion – approx. 30 x 20cm
Star cushion – approx. 30 x 30 cm

MATERIALS
Templates (see page 150)
0.5m cuddle soft or cotton
    print fabric per cushion
Felt scraps for appliqué details
Matching threads
Polyester toy stuffing

SUPPLIES
Paper or card for templates
Paper scissors
Fabric marker pen or tailor's chalk
Fabric scissors
Pins
Sewing machine and/or
    hand-sewing needle
Iron (if using cotton fabric)

STITCHES USED
Straight stitch
Zigzag or satin stitch
    (if sewing by machine)
Whipstitch (if sewing by hand)

TEMPLATES – see page 150
Cloud, star, moon templates,
    nursery cushion appliqué
    templates – cheek, eye/mouth,
    star eye, cloud mouth, moon eye

APPLIQUÉ THE FACE DETAILS

4. Working on each cushion in turn, take the front fabric piece and lay it on a flat surface with the right side facing up. Pin the relevant appliqué face details into position, using the photo opposite to guide you, and then sew into place. If sewing by hand, use a neat whipstitch or if sewing on the machine, use a zigzag or satin stitch.

FINISH THE CUSHIONS

5. Working on each cushion in turn, align the front and back fabric pieces with right sides facing together and pin in place. Stitch around the edge using a 1cm seam allowance and leaving a 4cm gap for turning.

6. Trim down seam allowances to 6mm, clipping corners and concave curves and notching convex curves. Turn right side out and smooth the seams by finger pressing into place. For cushions made from cotton fabric, press with an iron to neaten.

7. To finish, stuff the cushions with polyester toy stuffing, then hand stitch the opens seams closed with a neat whipstitch.

SLEEP SAFETY!
For small babies aged 0–6 months it is advised to keep cot accessories to a minimum and remove cushions from the crib if they are sleeping unattended.

QUILTED CRIB BUMPERS

Customise your baby's crib with some super-soft quilted bumper pads. I moved my daughter over from the bassinet to the cot at six months and decided bumpers were a personal must due to night-time acrobatics! Custom-made bumpers give you the opportunity to add your own touch as you can pick a fabric to match your nursery scheme or theme and play around with pattern and colour to create a cosy, co-ordinated crib for your baby.

This project makes a four-panel bumper set, which I've quilted to add some extra cosiness and texture. You can cover a set of ready-made baby bumper pads or make your own using some natural wadding. Remember to choose natural, breathable fabrics for both covering and filling your bumpers as it's important to maintain good airflow in the cot.

HOW TO PREPARE THE FABRICS AND TIES

1. Begin by cutting out the fabrics needed for all four bumpers. For the two large bumpers, measure and cut out four rectangles of fabric and two rectangles of wadding measuring 130 x 25cm. For the two small bumpers, measure and cut out four rectangles of fabric and two rectangles of wadding measuring 70 x 25cm. (Note that the bumpers shrink quite considerably once quilted. So the fabric and wadding should be cut larger and then cut down to the right size once quilted.)

2. Next, prepare the fabric ties. Measure and cut 20 strips of fabric measuring 60 x 8cm. (You could use contrasting fabric for this instead of the main bumper fabric.) Fold the first strip in half lengthwise with wrong sides together

continued on the next page

FINISHED SIZE

Suitable from 3 months old

2 Large bumpers – 120 x 25cm

2 Small bumpers – 65 x 25cm

* If your crib dimensions are different to mine, simply measure the perimeter of your baby's cot and alter to fit! *

MATERIALS

4m cotton fabric or fabrics

10m double-fold bias binding

Matching threads

1m high loft (thick) wadding
(approx. 3cm thick)

SUPPLIES

Fabric scissors

Pins

Measuring tape

Fabric marker pen or tailor's chalk

Sewing machine and/or
hand- sewing needle

Iron

STITCHES USED

Straight stitch

Zigzag stitch

and press. Unfold and bring both edges back into the middle to meet at the crease, again with wrong sides together, and press. Fold in the raw short edges by 0.5cm and press. Fold the strip in half again lengthwise to create a 1cm tie, then press. Repeat this process for the remaining strips until you have 20 folded and pressed ties.

3. Take a pressed fabric tie and pin the two long edges together. Use a straight stitch to sew the two short ends and along the open side, as close to the folded edges as possible. Repeat for each of the fabric ties and set them aside.

QUILT AND SEW THE BUMPERS

4. Take two of the large fabric rectangles and one of the large wadding rectangles. Lay the first fabric rectangle wrong side upwards on a flat surface, align the wadding on top and, finally, align the second fabric rectangle RIGHT side upwards to create a 'quilt sandwich'. Align all sides and pin the three layers together.

5. To quilt, sew vertical lines of stitching along the length of the bumper at regular intervals of approx. 10cm. The stitching lines should be parallel to the short sides. Use a quilting foot and an adjustable spacing bar, if you have them, to guide your stitching, or alternatively use a soluble fabric pen or tailor's chalk to mark out the lines before you sew. Use a long stitch and always start quilting from the centre out (sewing the first quilting line in the middle of the panel), alternating your stitching in opposite directions to prevent puckering and bunching.

6. Repeat steps 4 and 5 for the remaining three bumper panels.

7. Once quilted, measure the finished panels and cut down and square up all sides of the bumpers to the correct finished size.

8. Stitch around the perimeter of the bumper pads with a zigzag stitch. Finally, trim off loose threads ready for binding.

ATTACH THE BINDING

9. Take one of the large bumper panels and pin and stitch the binding into place around the perimeter of the pad. (See page 10 for binding how-to.)

10. Pin six ties to the inside edges of the bumper: one in each corner, 1cm in from the ends, and then one in the centre of each long side. Each tie should be pinned in the centre, so that the two ends will be free to tie to the cot.

11. Repeat steps 7–9 for the second long bumper pad. Repeat steps 7–9 for the two shorter pads, but omit the central ties.

12. Fix the finished bumpers onto the crib by tying the ties securely to the crib slats at each end of the bumper and in the middle of the two larger bumpers.

SAFETY! Keep cot accessories to a minimum in the first few months of a baby's life. Cot bumpers are not recommended to use until babies over 3 months old due to the potential risk of SIDS. It is also recommended that they are not used once babies can sit up unaided.

NURSING PILLOW

Nursing pillows are really useful both during pregnancy and after the baby is born. They help mums support their baby bump whilst sleeping and are great when mum and baby are nestled for nursing. I would have been totally lost without mine. As babies get older the pillow can be used to cushion them as they learn to sit upright. I created this cute and quirky kitty cushion to make a fun addition to your nursery – it would also make a super practical gift.

HOW TO CUT THE FABRICS

1. Using the template on page 152 as a guide, draw the nursing pillow onto paper or thin card. Photocopy or trace the nursing pillow ear and appliqué templates on page 152, enlarging them by the required percentage, onto paper or thin card. Cut out the templates with paper scissors.

2. Take your chosen cotton and fold the fabric in half lengthwise. Place the nursing pillow template near the top of the fabric with the fold line against the folded edge of the fabric. Mark the shape, then move the template down the fabric and mark out a second shape, again with the fold line against the fabric fold. Cut out both shapes – these are the front and back of the pillow. If you are using a directional pattern fabric, make sure the print runs the right way before marking and cutting.

3. Using the nursing pillow ear templates, mark and cut out two of each to create a front and a back for both the left and right ears.

4. Use the nursing pillow appliqué templates and the felt scraps to mark and cut out all of the facial features and

continued on the next page

FINISHED SIZE
Approx. 70 x 55cm

MATERIALS
Templates (see page 152)
2m cotton fabric
Felt scraps for appliqué details
Matching threads
2 x 250g bags of polyester toy
   stuffing

SUPPLIES
Paper or card for templates
Paper scissors
Fabric marker pen or tailor's chalk
Fabric scissors
Pins
Sewing machine and/or
   hand-sewing needle
Iron

STITCHES USED
Straight stitch
Zigzag stitch
Whipstitch

TEMPLATES – see page 152
Nursing pillow, nursing pillow ear,
   nursing pillow appliqué

inner ears. Follow the template guidelines for how many of each shape to mark and cut, and use the photo opposite as a guide as to colours.

APPLIQUÉ THE KITTY FACE

5. Referring to the photo opposite, position all the appliqué pieces except the inner ears onto the right side of one of the pillow pieces. The pupils sit on the eyes, the muzzle pieces overlap the tongue, the freckles sit on the muzzle and the nose overlaps the muzzle pieces.

6. Pin the felt pieces into position, then sew them in place using a straight or zigzag stitch. Where there is an overlap be sure to sew the underlying appliqué pieces first.

ASSEMBLE THE KITTY EARS

7. Place the felt inner ear appliqué shapes onto the centre front right sides of the cotton ear fabric pieces and pin in place. Stitch each one using a zigzag or straight stitch.

8. Pin the fabric ear pieces together, with right sides facing (one felt piece against one plain piece). Stitch around each ear using a 1cm seam allowance and leaving the bottom seam open for stuffing. Trim the seam allowance and turn the right sides out, poking the points of the ears out to sharp corners.

9. Stuff each ear with polyester toy stuffing and sew the open seam closed, with wrong sides together, using a zigzag stitch. Trim off any loose threads.

STITCH THE FRONT AND BACK PILLOW PIECES TOGETHER

10. Lay the appliquéd cushion front on a flat surface, with right side facing up. Position the ears along the top of the pillow above the cat's face, spaced evenly between the eyes and the whiskers (see photo opposite).

11. When you are happy with the ear position, flip each one downwards so that the bottom seam of each ear is sitting flush against the outside curve of the cat's head. Pin and then tack into place using a bright contrasting thread.

12. Lay the back piece of the pillow on top of the front and ears, with right sides facing and all edges aligned (ensure the kitty ears are sandwiched in between the two pieces). Pin in place and stitch around the edge of the pillow using a 1cm seam allowance, leaving an 8cm gap in the inside curve of the pillow.

13. Trim the seam allowance to 6mm, excluding the open seam, then clip around the outside curved edge and trim notches into the inside curve. Snip at the corners. Turn the right sides out and press, making sure you don't distort the felt.

STUFF AND FINISH THE PILLOW

14. Stuff the pillow with polyester toy stuffing, inserting as much as you like, depending on how firm or soft you prefer – but remember it should be firm enough to support your baby.

15. Once you've finished filling the pillow, fold the seam allowance of the opening inwards and hand-stitch the inside seam closed.

CHEVRON BABY QUILT

A handmade patchwork blanket is the ultimate labour of love for the little one in your life and this simple-to-sew quilt makes use of bright geometric shapes and the half-square triangle technique to create the classic chevron design. A unique style statement for any modern mum and baby, this cosy cot comforter is totally customisable. So feel free to mix it up and play around with the patterns, prints and colours or better yet why not re-purpose some treasured threads for some patchwork perfection?

My go-to baby gift of choice, this hand-sewn heirloom is sure to become a well-loved keepsake for many years to come. The seam allowance is 6mm due to the fractional measurements needed to cut out the squares along the diagonal.

HOW TO PREPARE THE FABRIC

1. Wash and press your fabrics before getting started. Photocopy or trace the square/triangle template on page 145, enlarging by the required percentage, onto paper or thin card. Cut out the template with paper scissors. Using the template, mark and cut out squares from the fabrics as follows:

   - ◕ Fabrics A and B: 15 squares each
   - ◕ Fabrics C and D: 12 squares each

2. Prepare the squares for sewing by pairing them using the layout diagram on page 145 and the photos as a guide.

continued on the next page

FINISHED SIZE
90 x 60cm

MATERIALS
Square template (see page 145)
0.5m fabric in colour A, 15 squares
0.5m fabric in colour B, 15 squares
0.25m fabric in colour C, 12 squares
0.25m fabric in colour D, 12 squares
1m cotton backing fabric
1m natural fibre quilt wadding
4m double-fold bias binding
Matching threads

SUPPLIES
Paper or card for template
Paper scissors
Ruler
Fabric marker pen or tailor's chalk
Rotary cutter and mat or
    fabric scissors
Pins
Sewing machine
Iron

STITCHES USED
Straight stitch

TEMPLATES – see page 145
12.2cm square

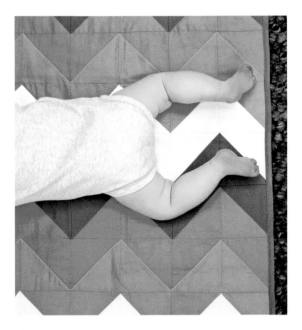

3. Place pairs together as follows, keeping right sides together and aligning edges:

- 🏀 9 x A and B
- 🏀 6 x B and C
- 🏀 6 x C and D
- 🏀 6 x A and D

4. The quilt is constructed using half-square triangles – squares made up of two right-angled triangles. It's a super simple patchwork technique and loads of fun to make once you get the hang of it. To sew a half-square triangle, take your first pair of squares and pin together with right sides facing, then use a ruler and a fabric pen to mark out a diagonal line from one corner to the opposite corner onto the wrong side of one of the fabric squares.

5. Using the marked line as a guide, sew a seam 6mm from the line on either side of it, parallel to the guide line. Then cut along the guide line and open out the two pieces created to reveal two half-square triangles.

6. Repeat steps 3 and 4 for the remaining 26 pairs to give you the 54 half-square triangle units needed to complete the quilt.

7. Press the seams towards the darker fabric on the back of each square, then lightly press again on the front of each fabric square for a neat finish. Trim off all the little corner 'dog ears' to create a perfect square. Finished half-square triangle squares should measure 10 x 10cm.

continued on the next page

SEW THE SQUARES TO CREATE THE CHEVRON BANDS

8. To create the repeated zigzag bands you will need to arrange the half-square triangle blocks to form the pattern. Arrange the squares into nine strips of six following the layout diagram on page 145.

9. Join the pieces for row 1 – pin and sew the squares with right sides facing using a precise 6mm seam allowance. Be careful to match up the corner seams as neatly as possible as this will help keep your pattern accurate and exact. Press the seams open as you go along.

10. Repeat step 9 until all of the rows are joined together and you have nine strips. Now you can start joining the strips together to complete the zigzag chevron pattern. Pin and then stitch the strips with right sides together, following the layout diagram (see page 145) and, again, using a precise 6mm seam allowance. Make sure you align the seams that join each square as you sew to ensure a perfect pattern.

11. Press the seams open and then, finally, press the front of the quilt top to neaten.

ASSEMBLE THE QUILT

12. Press and then lay out the backing fabric on a flat surface with the wrong side facing upwards. Lay the quilt wadding on top, so that at least one side aligns. Finally lay the quilt top on top of the two layers with the right side facing upwards, leaving approx. 5cm of wadding and backing fabric sticking out all around.

13. Working from the centre outwards, pin or tack the three layers together at intervals of approx. 15cm to hold the assembled quilt together. Hand or machine stitch straight lines where the rows of blocks meet. This is known as quilting in the ditch.

14. Remove any pins and tacking threads and trim the quilt edges so that they are straight and the corners are square.

15. To finish the quilt, use matching or contrasting double-fold bias binding tape to encase the raw edges of the quilt. (See page 10 for information on binding techniques.)

BABY SLUMBER SACK

Baby slumber sacks provide comfort, warmth and peace of mind for parents as these wearable blankets help keep babies cosy during the night and at naptimes. My daughter lived in hers for the first year of her life and we would have been lost without one. Slumber sacks can be made to suit any climate depending on what fabrics you use; I have chosen a snuggly bamboo cotton fleece for an easy-to-wear medium, winter-weight version.

HOW TO CUT THE FABRICS

1. Photocopy or trace the slumber sack back, front, front facing and back facing templates on page 158, enlarging by the required percentage, onto paper or thin card. Cut out the templates with paper scissors.

2. Before cutting, lay all the templates onto the fabric following the fabric cutting guide on page 159. Both sizes need to be cut on double thickness fabric. Fold the fabric right sides together and if you're using a fabric with a pile or nap (such as fleece), fold the fabric crosswise.

3. Pin the front template onto the fabric (the template includes extra seam allowance along the inside middle seam for the zip). Cut out four on double thickness fabric to create two pairs of front body pieces – one pair from the outer fabric and one pair from the lining.

4. Use the back body template to cut out one back piece from the outer fabric. To do so, fold the fabric in half, selvedge to selvedge, with the stretchiest part of the fabric on the fold. Cut the back piece against the fold of the fabric.

continued on the next page

SIZES
0–6 months
6–12 months

MATERIALS
Templates (see page 158)
2m organic cotton bamboo fleece or fabric of your choice for both outer fabric and lining
Matching threads
55cm polyester zip
2 pairs of 18mm sew-on snap fasteners

SUPPLIES
Paper or card for templates
Paper scissors
Fabric marker pen or tailor's chalk
Fabric scissors
Pins
Sewing machine and/or hand-sewing needle
Ball point stretch needle (if using stretch fabric and a sewing machine)

STITCHES USED
Straight stitch
Zigzag stitch
Whipstitch
Slipstitch

TEMPLATES – see page 158
Slumber sack front, back, front facing and back facing

5. Use the back facing and front facing templates to cut out one front facing and one back facing piece, cutting along the fold of the fabric.

6. Cut the notches on the fabric pieces, approx. 5mm in from the edge, to help with matching the seams.

SEW THE SACK

7. Stitch along the bottom seam of the back facing piece using zigzag stitch to prevent the raw edge from fraying.

8. Pin the back body and back facing pieces together with right sides facing and all edges aligned. Stitch around the armhole seam, all the way around the neck and finish at the other armhole seam – do not sew the side seams together yet. Trim down the facing side of the seam allowance to approx. 4mm. Clip around the curves of the seam and turn right sides out.

9. Lay the armhole seam open and flat with the seam allowance turned towards the facing side of the sack. Topstitch around the seam edge of the armhole curve onto the front right side of the facing fabric, approx. 2mm in from the seam, for approx. 10cm. Repeat for the opposite armhole and back of the neck.

10. Fold the front facing piece in half along the fold line, with right sides facing inwards, and stitch together leaving the long straight seam open. Trim the seam allowance and clip the curved seam as close to the stitching line as possible to reduce the thickness of the fabric. Turn right sides out.

11. Place the open seam of the front facing piece flush against the top CF seam, approx. 1cm in from the edge of one of the front body lining pieces, with right sides together. Stitch into place with a 1cm seam allowance. This will create the flap to sit in front of the zip.

SEW THE ZIP AND JOIN THE FRONT AND BACK PIECES

12. Sandwich one side of the zip tape between the front body and the lining so that the zip is facing the right side of the front body and the back of the zip is facing the right side of the lining. Using a zip foot attachment, stitch all the way down the CF seam to the bottom of the sack, joining the zip to both body pieces and moving the zip pull out of the way as you stitch

along the tape. Trim the facing side of the seam allowance to approx. 4mm. Repeat with the opposite side of the zip and the opposite side of the front body outer piece and lining.

13. To continue joining the front body outer fabric and lining pieces, stitch around the armhole, neck and strap seams on both sides – do not sew the seams together yet. Trim the lining side of the seam allowance to 4mm and clip into the seam allowance around the curves to reduce bulk. Turn right sides out, lay the armhole seams open and flat and topstitch approx. 2mm in from the lining side of the seam for approx. 10cm. Repeat for the other side of the front body and lining.

14. Place the front and back pieces together with right sides of the fabric facing and front lining and back facing right sides together. Stitch along the side seams down to the double notches. Trim the seam allowance and clip into the curved seam. At the double notch, trim the seam at a 90-degree angle towards the open seam in the direction of the CF. Repeat for the opposite side of the front body and back body. Using the open seams at the bottom of the sack, turn right sides out.

15. To close the slumber sack, fold under the open seams to the inside of the bag and secure with a straight stitch. Finish off the raw edges with a zigzag stitch to prevent them from fraying. If sewing by hand, secure with a slipstitch.

16. Use the marker points on the templates to position and stitch a pair of snap fasteners onto each strap of the slumber sack to secure. See page 11 for how to sew on snap fasteners.

RAINCLOUD & THUNDERCLOUD MOBILES

Brighten up your baby's nursery with some whimsical handmade hanging art. Traditionally hung above the crib, mobiles also look sweet strung up beside a baby changing station or simply displayed as a wall decoration around the nursery. Rainclouds and lightning bolts have become a big design trend and make a quirky addition to any baby's new boudoir. Use a selection of brightly coloured felts to help captivate and stimulate your baby's developing eyesight. This mesmerising mobile is a super-quick and inexpensive project and can easily be sewn either on the machine or by hand with a neat and nifty blanket stitch.

HOW TO MAKE A RAINCLOUD MOBILE

1. Using the templates on page 147 as a guide, draw the cloud and raindrop templates onto paper or thin card. Cut out each template with paper scissors. Use the cloud template to cut out two clouds in white felt. Use the raindrop template to cut out 18 raindrops to make nine double-sided raindrops in a variety of colours. You can use the colour suggestions in the photo opposite or choose your own palette to suit the nursery style and décor.

2. Stitch the two felt cloud pieces together, either on the machine or by hand using a small straight stitch and a 1cm seam allowance or blanket stitch 1cm from the edge. Leave one rounded edge open for stuffing.

3. Fill the cloud with the polyester stuffing, then pin and stitch the open seam closed. Do the same for the raindrops, leaving the bottom edge open to fill with just enough stuffing to hold their shape, then pin and stitch the open seams closed.

continued on the next page

SIZE
Approx. 43 x 63cm
Suitable from birth

MATERIALS
Templates (see page 147)
0.5m white felt and grey felt
   for each raincloud
0.25m yellow felt for lightning bolt
Selection of felt scraps in a variety
   of colours for the raindrops
Matching threads
Polyester toy stuffing
Fishing wire or strong embroidery
   thread plus a hook, for hanging

SUPPLIES
Paper or card for templates
Paper scissors
Fabric marker pen or tailor's chalk
Fabric scissors
Pins
Sewing machine and/or
   hand-sewing needle

STITCHES USED
Straight stitch
Blanket stitch (optional)

TEMPLATES – see page 147
Cloud (both designs), lightning bolt
   (thundercloud only), raindrop
   (raincloud only)

4. Assemble the mobile using fishing wire and a needle. Thread a needle with the wire and attach through the top of the cloud, knotting into place against the stitching line edge. Tie the ends of the fishing wire securely to create a loop and hang from a nail or hook in the wall.

5. Use extra fishing wire or embroidery thread to join and hang the felt raindrops together. Thread the needle with a long length of fishing wire approx. 40cm long. Make a knot against the bottom stitching line edge of the first raindrop by threading the needle through the raindrop from the bottom, bringing the needle up and out through the top pointed end of the raindrop. Leave 2–3 cm of wire before attaching another raindrop by knotting the wire against the bottom stitching line edge as before. Continue to attach raindrops onto the wire at intervals by threading and knotting into place as described as above. Use the photo opposite as a guide for layout spacing. Secure the raindrop strands into place by knotting into position against the bottom stitching line edge of the raincloud. Trim off any loose ends.

HOW TO MAKE A THUNDERCLOUD MOBILE

1. Using the templates on page 147 as a guide, draw the cloud and lightning bolt onto paper or thin card. Cut out each template with paper scissors. Use the cloud template and cut out two in dark grey felt. Use the lightning bolt template to cut out two in yellow felt.

2. Pin the matching felt pieces together and stitch around the outline, either on the machine or by hand using a small straight stitch and a 1cm seam allowance or blanket stitch 1cm from the edge. Leave an open seam on each shape for stuffing. Fill the shapes with just enough stuffing to hold their shape, then pin and stitch the open seams closed to finish.

3. Assemble the mobile using fishing wire in the same way as for the raincloud, this time attaching the thunderbolt under the cloud instead of the raindrops (see photo on page 37).

If you like a bit of wit and whimsy why not add a cute face to the front of your cloud with some small scraps of felt or put your needle to good use and embroider a cheerful expression to delight and amuse!

APPLIQUÉ ONESIES

Give your babe a fresh, hip look every day of the week with your own self-styled baby wear. Appliqué is one of the easiest ways to customise baby gear from onesies and muslins to blankets and beyond. Baby onesies are a style staple, and customising and embellishing them is not only fun but also easy.

Appliqué is the simple technique of applying cut-out fabric shapes and designs onto a fabric background, securing into place with stitches either sewn by hand or on the machine. I like using the iron-on fusible web technique best, as all you need are a few templates, a bit of fusible web and some snazzy zigzag stitching. Make up your own slogans, hand-draw your own designs or, for easy foolproof sewing, photocopy and cut out mine to create your own personalised graphic baby wear. I made masses of these for my own babe. You can update their style as often as they outgrow their clothes for a designer look on a shoestring budget!

HOW TO

1. Photocopy or trace the template you have chosen to use from page 141 onto paper or thin card. Alternatively, design your own shape or slogan and draw it onto paper or thin card. Cut out the template with paper scissors.

2. Preheat your iron to a medium heat setting – no steam! Draw around your chosen template shape on the paper backing side of the fusible web. If your design is directional, make sure you flip the template over and draw around it in reverse. Roughly cut around the shape leaving a border of at least 1cm.

continued on the next page

SIZES
3–6 months
6–9 months

MATERIALS
Templates (see page 141)
Paper-backed fusible web (I use Bondaweb or HeatnBond Lite)
Cotton fabric scraps for appliqué
Plain baby onesies
Matching thread

SUPPLIES
Paper or card for templates
Iron
Paper scissors
Fabric scissors
Sewing machine and/or hand-sewing needle
Ball point stretch needle (if using sewing machine)

STITCHES USED
Zigzag or satin stitch (if sewing by machine)
Whipstitch or blanket stitch (if sewing by hand)

TEMPLATES – see page 141
Choice of designs for either 3–6 months or 6–9 months sizes.

3. Place the webbing template adhesive-side down (paper side up) onto the wrong side of your chosen appliqué fabric and press with an iron to fuse the webbing into place. Press for 2–5 seconds at a time, overlapping the areas you press and making sure that you press each part of the design until the entire surface has bonded.

4. Repeat steps 1–3 for any additional shapes or designs you want to use. Cut out each shape from the fused web and cotton appliqué fabric.

5. Remove the fusible webbing paper by peeling it off to reveal a sticky backing, and place the appliqué shape, sticky-side down, into position onto the front right side of the onesie. Press and hold the iron onto the design for 5–10 seconds until each section of the appliqué is bonded to the fabric background, and then leave to cool, ready for stitching.

6. To sew by hand, us a neat whipstitch or blanket stitch and either matching or contrasting thread to sew around the edges of the shapes.

7. To sew on the machine, use a ballpoint stretch needle and a small zigzag or satin stitch to completely cover the raw edges of the appliqué shapes by following the outlines of the designs.

Make sure you wash your home-sewn appliqué inside out, on a cold and gentle wash. Always pre-wash and iron all fabrics before stitching your appliqué.

BABY BATH TOWEL

Another baby essential to check off your must-have list is a snuggly bath towel. These are so simple and easy to make yourself, you can either re-purpose an existing household towel if you're feeling thrifty or pick out a brand new bath sheet or piece of towelling fabric for a pretty but practical baby shower gift. Attach some ears for a cute finish!

HOW TO CUT THE FABRIC

1. Photocopy or trace the ear template on page 150 onto paper or thin card. Cut out the template with paper scissors and put to one side.

2. Cut a 75cm square from both the towelling and fleece fabrics. Align them with right sides together and pin.

3. For the hood, cut out a right-angled triangle with the two equal sides measuring 35cm in length from both the towelling and the fleece fabrics.

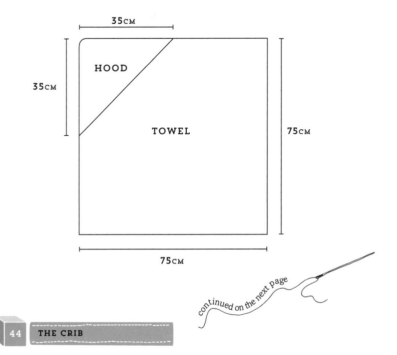

SIZE
75 x 75cm
Suitable from birth

MATERIALS
Template (see page 150)
1m towelling fabric or a
    large bath sheet
1m fleece fabric
Matching threads

SUPPLIES
Paper or card for templates
Paper scissors
Tape measure
Fabric marker pen or tailor's chalk
Fabric scissors
Pins
Sewing machine and/or
    hand-sewing needle

STITCHES USED
Straight stitch
Zigzag stitch

TEMPLATES – see page 150
Ears – cut out four

continued on the next page

MAKE AND POSITION THE EARS

4. Use the ear template to cut out four ear shapes using the remaining fleece fabric. Align two pieces with right sides facing and sew together using a 1cm seam allowance, leaving the bottom seam open. Trim the seam allowance, then turn the right side out. Repeat for the second ear.

5. Position the ears in place on the front right side of the fleece hood approx. 10cm apart. Cut a small slit approx. 2cm long into the hood at each ear position. Poke the ears into the slits and pin the bottom open seams into place on the underside of the hood. Stitch down using a small zigzag stitch in matching threads.

SEW THE HOOD

6. Place the fleece and the towelling hood pieces on top of each other with right sides together. Align all edges. Pin along the long edge of the hood (this will be the bottom seam) and stitch into place using a 1cm seam allowance.

7. Fold the hood over itself so that both right sides of the fabric are now facing outside and wrong sides are together. Topstitch along the bottom seam to add stability to the front of the hood.

ATTACH THE HOOD TO THE TOWEL

8. To stitch the hood into the main towel, you need to sandwich it in between the fleece and towelling layers at one corner of the square towel. Unpin a corner, then place the hood with the right side facing up on top of the towelling side of the square. Align all edges of the hood.

9. Fold the fleece back over and on top of the hood and realign all edges, re-pinning the corner as before.

10. Round off the top corner point of both the towel and the hood to create a curved corner edge. Use a round object such as a plate or a bowl to give you the correct angle. Trim off the corner point, then pin.

11. Stitch 1cm around all edges of the towel leaving a 15cm gap for turning right side out. Clip the corners and trim down the seam allowance, being careful not to cut through the stitching.

12. Turn the towel right side out. Topstitch 1cm in from the edge on all sides, excluding the hood, and catching the open seam closed as you sew to finish.

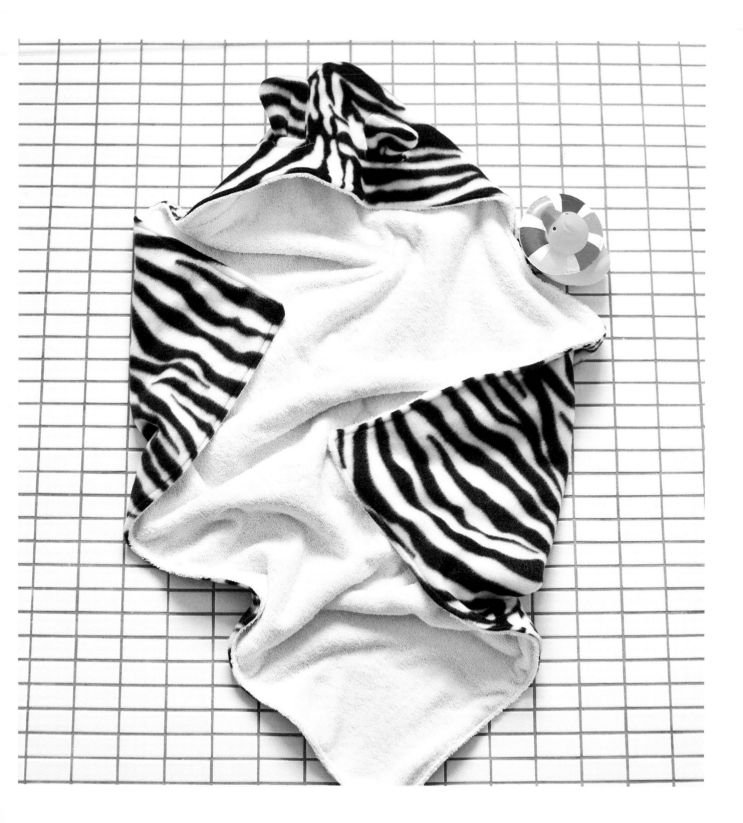

BABY SCRAPBOOK

A custom-made fabric-covered scrapbook will make a thoughtful keepsake for any new mum to be. To make your own handcrafted covering, buy a brand new notebook or photo album or cover an existing shop-bought baby book ready for parents to fill with their best baby photos, doodles and words to record those all-important milestone moments. For a personal touch choose a favourite fabric, perhaps even something meaningful for mum, then add some appliqué details or quilt it to make a handmade heirloom to treasure in the years to come.

HOW TO CUT THE FABRIC

1. If you are using them, photocopy or trace the book appliqué design templates on pages 154–155 onto paper or thin card. Cut out the templates with paper scissors. Set aside.

2. Iron the fabric so it is wrinkle free and ready for cutting and sewing.

3. Measure the height and length of your scrapbook to determine the amount of fabric you will need to cut for the front and back covering. The best way to do this is to wrap a tape measure around the closed book. Take note of the dimensions from sides and spine, then adding on extra for two folded flaps that will cover approx. three-quarters of the inside front and inside back covers of the book. Once you have these dimensions you will need to add on extra for seam allowance on all sides. As a general rule, add on 2cm at each short end and 3cm top and bottom to allow for extra bulkiness and topstitching, too.

continued on the next page

MATERIALS

Templates (see pages 154–155
    – optional)
Hardback notebook or photo album
1m cotton fabric or 2 x 0.5m pieces
    of contrasting cotton fabric
Felt scraps for the appliqué
    (optional)
0.5m lightweight polyester wadding
Matching threads

SUPPLIES

Paper or card for templates
    (if using)
Paper scissors (if using templates)
Iron
Tape measure
Fabric marker pen or tailor's chalk
Fabric scissors
Pins
Sewing machine and/or
    hand-sewing needle

STITCHES USED

Straight stitch
Zigzag stitch (if using machine)
Blanket or whipstitch (if hand
    sewing)

TEMPLATES – see
    pages 154–155
Book appliqué design (optional)

4. Using these measurements, cut out two identical fabric rectangles – one for the book cover outside and one for the book cover inside. You can choose to have the fabrics either matching or contrasting.

5. Cut out one rectangle of wadding the same size as the book cover outside.

ASSEMBLE AND SEW THE BOOK COVER

6. Lay the book cover inside fabric face up on a flat surface. Place the book cover outside fabric on top with right side facing downwards and all edges aligned with the book cover inside. Place the wadding rectangle on top of the two layers, again with all edges aligned, and pin the three layers together.

7. Sew around all sides of the three layers using a 1cm seam allowance and a straight stitch. Leave a 6cm gap for turning in the middle of one of the long edges. Trim the seam allowance, including the extra wadding, clip the corners then, turn the right sides out. Press to neaten with an iron, tucking in the open seam and pressing into place.

8. Lay down the book cover with the inside fabric facing up. Fold over each end towards the inside of the cover to form folded flap pockets. Refer to the measurements you took in step 3 to determine how much of each side to fold over. Press and pin in place.

9. Topstitch 0.5cm from the edge along the top and bottom edges of the book cover, catching the open seam and the folded and pinned flap pockets into place as you sew.

10. Attach the finished soft cover to your hardback book by inserting the hardback cover into the flap pockets of your handmade soft cover.

APPLIQUÉ THE BOOK COVER FRONT

11. If you want to appliqué the front, using the templates from step 1, pin, mark and cut out the appliqué designs in contrasting coloured felt.

12. Position the appliqués onto the right side of the book cover front fabric in the front cover area, referring to the measurements you took in step 3, and pin into place. Stitch the appliqué pieces using matching threads and a small zigzag stitch, if using a sewing machine or, if sewing by hand, use a neat blanket or whipstitch.

BABES IN THE HOOD

OUT AND ABOUT WITH BABY

Keep your baby stitched in style with my collection of baby clothes and accessories that are as affordable and fun to sew as they are practical! Going out and about with your baby will require a few handy essentials to make those trips just that little bit easier – try your hand at some simple-to-sew baby bandana bibs to take care of messy mealtimes, and never lose another dummy again with some nifty DIY dummy clips. Or make your own on-the-go baby-changing essentials with a portable travel changing mat and matching nappy clutch bag to fold-and-go in style. And keep babies both cosy and cute with some hand-stitched clothing and heirlooms – choose a bright modern baby bonnet that is perfect for pram rides or stitch up a pair of fun but functional dungarees. Not forgetting my favourites – a pair of soft felt moccasins, the perfect first shoes for tiny trendsetting tots!

BLANKEY BUDDY

Make a snuggly-soft blanket buddy like this cute comforter for your new arrival. Stitch it up in some ultra-soft and totally huggable plush fabrics using high-contrast colours such as black and white, which babies love – a perfect excuse to make a panda bear pal for your baby! This project is brilliant for making use of leftover fabrics from your stash but also makes a lovely, luxurious gift that is perfect for a baby to carry around to soothe and comfort them.

HOW TO CUT THE FABRIC

1. Photocopy or trace the panda arms, head and face details templates on page 148 onto paper or thin card. Cut out the templates with paper scissors.

2. Measure and cut out two squares of matching or contrasting soft fabric for the blanket, each measuring 41 x 41cm. I used a mixture of minky and cuddle soft plush in black and white.

3. Use the panda head and face detail templates to mark and cut out two panda heads in a cuddly soft fabric, four ears, two eyes, the nose and the mouth in a mix of felt offcuts.

4. Use the panda arms template to mark and cut out two pieces in black felt.

SEW THE BLANKET

5. Place the two 41cm squares of fabric on top of each other with all edges aligned and right sides of the fabric facing together. Pin together and stitch around all edges with a 0.5cm seam allowance, leaving a 6cm gap down one of the sides. Trim the seam allowance and clip the corners, then turn the blanket right sides out.

continued on the next page

FINISHED SIZE
40 x 40cm

MATERIALS
Templates (see page 148)

1m fabric in total for the blanket – use a mix of something soft and snuggly such as teddy soft faux fur, fleece, minky or chenille for either side for added texture and contrast

12.5cm cuddle soft fabric for panda head

Felt scraps for appliqué features and face details

12.5cm black fleece for panda arms

Matching threads plus some strong sewing thread

Polyester toy stuffing

SUPPLIES
Paper or card for templates

Paper scissors

Fabric marker pen or tailor's chalk

Fabric scissors

Pins

Sewing machine and/or hand-sewing needle

STITCHES USED
Straight stitch

Zigzag stitch

TEMPLATES – see page 148
Panda arms, head and face details

6. Poke the corners out into sharp points and tuck the opening's seam allowance under. Topstitch around the edges using a straight stitch as close to the edge as possible, catching the open part of the seam closed as you do so.

ASSEMBLE, JOIN AND SEW THE PANDA HEAD AND ARMS

7. Start with the appliqué details for the panda face. Stitch the two eye components together using the photo on page 57 as a guide to placement. Now sew the eyes onto the front right side of the fabric face. Do the same for the nose and the mouth, stitching them into place with matching threads and a zigzag stitch.

8. Pin the ear pieces, with right sides together, in pairs and sew using a zigzag stitch, leaving the bottom seam edges open. Turn them right sides out and stuff with just enough polyester toy stuffing to give them some shape. Close the bottom seams with a zigzag stitch.

9. Pin the ears into place onto the front right side of the panda face, positioning them so that the bottom seams lay flush against the top outside edge of the head. Place the back of the panda head on top of the front with right sides of the fabric facing together and all edges aligned. The ears should be sandwiched between the head front and back, pointing inwards. Pin and then stitch using a 0.5cm seam allowance, catching the ears as you sew and leaving a 3cm gap at the bottom of the head. Trim off any extra seam allowance and turn the head right sides

out. Stuff with polyester toy stuffing, adding in a plastic squeaker (if using) and hand-stitch the open seam closed with a neat whipstitch. Set aside.

10. Sew the arm pieces together. To do so, align them with right sides of the fabric facing together. Pin and then stitch using 0.5cm seam allowance and leave a 3cm gap in the middle. Trim and notch the seam allowance, then turn the arms right sides out. Stuff with polyester toy stuffing until firm. Hand-stitch the open seam closed with a neat whipstitch.

ASSEMBLE AND FINISH THE BLANKET

11. Join the panda head to the panda arms so that the head is sitting on top of the arms, securing into place with a neat and sturdy hand stitch using some strong matching thread.

12. Find the centre point of the blanket. Pin the panda arms and head into place and stitch securely through the two blanket layers using matching strong thread.

Add a plastic squeaker so the panda makes a noise when squeezed!

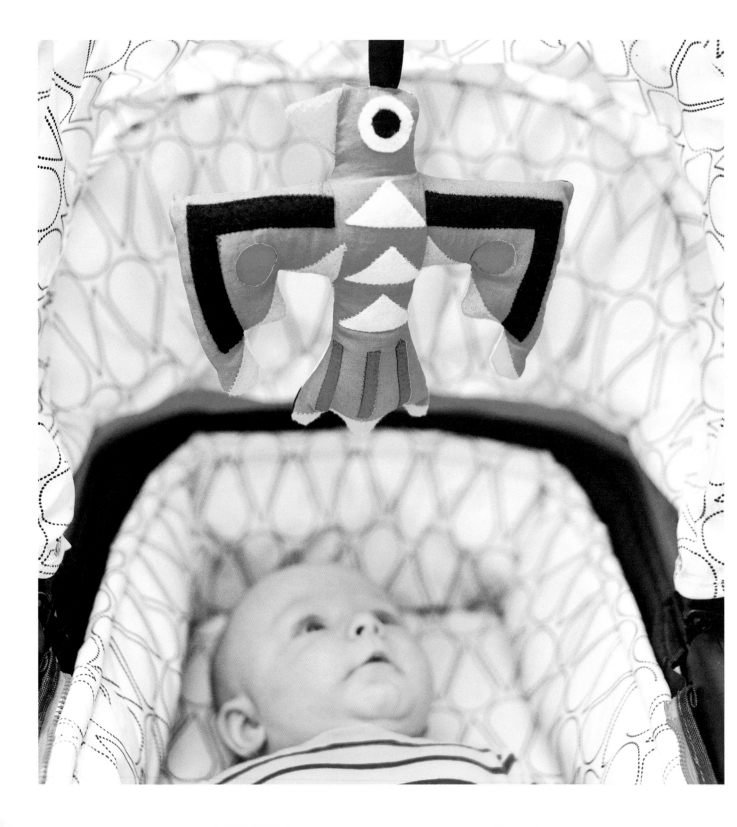

DIY PRAM TOY

A bright and colourful clip-on travel toy is the ultimate on-the-go accessory to keep babies amused and entertained while you're out and about. My daughter Bou absolutely loved hers and this quirky character can be clipped onto the pram, the car seat or the crib. Stuff with a rattle insert, a squeaker or some crinkly paper and attach a fabric strap onto some plastic link clips and rings that help babies keep favourite toys close to hand.

HOW TO CUT THE FABRIC

1. Photocopy or trace the bird body, beak and appliqué templates on page 151, enlarging by the required percentage, onto paper or thin card. Cut out the templates with paper scissors.

2. Fold the cotton fabric so that the bird body template fits onto two layers of the fabric with its edge on the fold as marked on the template. Mark the shape and cut out. Repeat to create a second bird body shape. Use the bird beak templates to mark and cut out two beak shapes from yellow felt and set aside.

3. Use the bird appliqué templates to pin, mark and cut out all the details in a variety of contrasting felts. Use the photo opposite as a guide.

4. Take the front bird piece and lay it, with the right side facing up, on a flat surface. Pin the felt pieces into place, again using the photo opposite as a guide. Begin by stitching the pupil to the eye, and then stitch all felt pieces into place using matching threads and a small zigzag stitch.

5. Take the two bird beak pieces and pin them together with the right sides facing and all edges aligned. Stitch together, using a 0.5cm seam allowance and a straight stitch, leaving

FINISHED SIZE
22cm wide

MATERIALS
Template (see page 151)
0.25m cotton fabric
Selection of coloured felt pieces
Matching threads
Polyester toy stuffing

SUPPLIES
Paper or card for templates
Paper scissors
Fabric marker pen or tailor's chalk
Fabric scissors
Pins
Sewing machine
Iron
Hand-sewing needle

STITCHES USED
Straight stitch
Zigzag stitch
Whipstitch

TEMPLATES – see page 151
Bird body, beak, appliqué

continued on the next page

the bottom seam open. Clip the corners and trim the seam allowance, then turn the right sides out. Stuff with a small piece of polyester toy stuffing, then zigzag stitch the open seam closed.

MAKE THE FABRIC TIE

6. See the Baby Bow Tie on page 99 for instructions on how to make a fabric tie. Use either some of the remaining cotton fabric from the bird body or choose a contrasting colour. Once prepared and sewn, set aside to be stitched into the bird body.

SEW THE BIRD FRONT AND BACK

7. Pin the bird beak into position on the right side of the appliquéd bird front, placing the bottom seam flush against the seam edge of the bird head with the beak facing inwards on top of the head (it will be flipped outwards once sewn). Fold the fabric tie in half lengthwise and place the two open ends of the tie flush against the seam edge of the bird front at the top of the bird's head with the fabric loop facing inwards (again, this will be flipped outwards once sewn). This will become the fabric strap you can use for displaying the bird once finished.

8. Pin the bird back piece on top of the front with right sides of the fabrics facing together and the bird beak and fabric tie sandwiched in between the two layers, aligning all edges carefully. Stitch together using a straight stitch and a 0.5cm seam allowance. Make sure you follow all the sharp edges and angles of the bird

outline as you sew. Leave a 6cm gap for turning on one of the long straight edges.

9. Clip the corners, trim seam allowance and turn the right sides out, making sure you poke all corners out into sharp points. Press on the back of the bird to neaten.

10. Stuff with polyester toy stuffing until all corners are filled and the bird is nice and firm. If you want to include a rattle or squeaker, place it inside the bird so that it sits in the centre, surrounded by filling.

11. Hand-sew the open seam closed with some matching thread and a neat whipstitch.

TRAVEL CHANGING MAT

A portable, foldaway travel mat is an absolute must-have for changing babies on the go. This compact, lightweight mat is the perfect size to fit into any handbag and makes a stylish set paired up with the Nappy Clutch on pages 69–71. I would have been lost without both of these essential bits of baby kit, as every mum wants to make sure her baby has somewhere clean and comfy to be changed when out and about. I made mine with an easy wipe-clean lightweight vinyl and a layer of wadding for some soft padding.

HOW TO

1. Using the dimensions diagram (see page 66) as a guide, measure and mark the shape onto the back of your cotton outer fabric, wadding and vinyl lining fabric. Cut out all three shapes.

2. To define the fold lines and add some extra cushioning, the travel changing mat outer fabric and wadding can be quilted together using matching threads and a long straight stitch. Pin the cotton and the wadding pieces together with the right side of the cotton facing outwards. Using the measurements given in the diagram on page 66 follow the stitching lines to quilt, working from the centre outwards.

3. Pin the vinyl lining fabric to the quilted mat top with wrong sides of the fabric together (vinyl against the wadding) and stitch all the way around the edges using a 0.5cm seam allowance.

4. To encase the raw edges of the travel mat use double-fold bias binding to finish off the open seams. (See the binding how-to on page 10.)

continued on the next page

SIZE
Suitable from birth

MATERIALS
1m cotton fabric
1m lightweight wadding
1m vinyl lining fabric
Matching threads
3m double-fold bias binding
1 pair of 18mm sew-on snap
    fasteners

SUPPLIES
Tape measure
Ruler
Fabric marker pen or tailor's chalk
Fabric scissors
Pins
Sewing machine
Hand-sewing needle

STITCHES USED
Straight stitch
Whipstitch

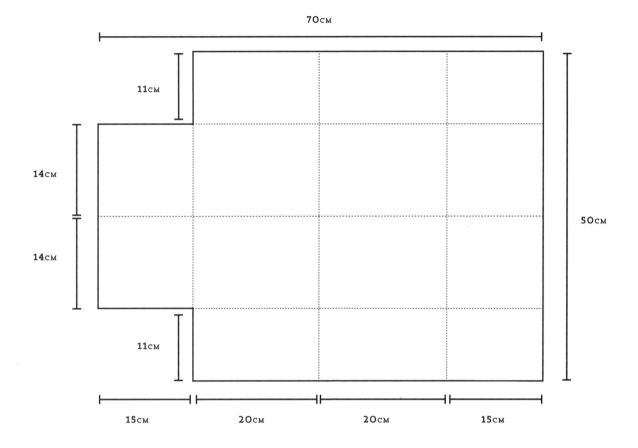

70cm

11cm

14cm

14cm

11cm

50cm

15cm   20cm   20cm   15cm

5. Fold up the mat by bringing both long sides in to meet in the middle. Then roll and fold the mat, using the quilting lines as guides, towards the protruding rectangle to create a folded flap at the front. This is where you will need to secure the popper snap.

6. Attach a sew-on snap fastner to the folded mat with the stud part of the snap on the inside

lining at the top centre of the flap. Hand stitch with a neat and secure whipstitch. Stitch the socket part of the snap onto the front right side of the mat at the point where it will comfortably meet the stud, again with a neat and secure whipstitch.

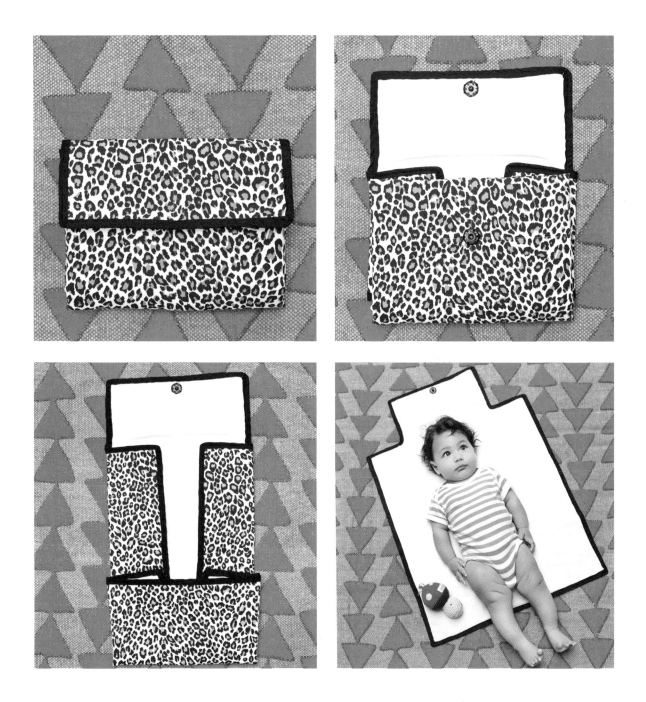

NAPPY CLUTCH

Keep your own handbag clutter free with this neat and tidy nappy clutch, perfect for carrying around your baby-changing essentials. This nifty bag unfolds to reveal two handy slip pockets with just enough space for nappies and wipes. I never left the house without mine! Make one to match the Travel Changer Mat on pages 64–67 to stitch your own set of grab-and-go baby travel accessories.

HOW TO

1. Measure, mark and cut out a rectangle measuring 70 x 28cm from your outer cotton print fabric, another from your lining fabric and a third from your wadding.

2. Align the outer fabric and the lining fabric with right sides facing. Place the rectangle of wadding behind the two layers, aligning all edges again, and pin into place.

3. Stitch the three layers together by sewing around all sides using a straight stitch and a 1cm seam allowance, leaving a 6cm gap for turning along the middle of one of the long sides. This is where you will eventually place your hand strap.Clip the corners, then turn the right sides out, making sure you poke the corners out into sharp points.

4. Measure, mark and cut out a strip of outer cotton print fabric measuring 6 x 22cm. Fold in half lengthwise with wrong sides facing and press.

5. Unfold the strip, then bring both long raw edges in to meet at the middle crease. Press again. Finally fold in half

FINISHED SIZE
Unfolded – 36cm x 25cm
Folded – 18cm x 25cm

MATERIALS
0.5m cotton print fabric
0.5m lining fabric
0.5m low-loft, lightweight wadding
Matching threads
1 x pair of 18mm sew-on snap
   fasteners (optional)

SUPPLIES
Tape measure
Fabric marker pen or tailor's chalk
Fabric scissors
Pins
Sewing machine
Hand-sewing needle
Iron

STITCHES USED
Straight stitch
Whipstitch

continued on the next page

lengthwise along the initial crease to create a hand strap measuring 1.5cm in width. Press and stitch all the way along the open edge to secure.

6. Fold the hand strap in half to create a loop and position the raw ends into the open seam used for turning out the nappy clutch and pin into place.

7. Fold the two short ends of the padded rectangle inwards by 16cm at either side. This should create two folded inside pockets with a 4cm gap in the middle (see diagram below right). Pin into place.

8. Using matching thread, topstitch 0.5cm in from the edge around the perimeter of the whole bag, catching both the hand strap and the open seam closed as you sew.

9. Stitch a pair of sew-on snap fasteners at either inside edge of the unfolded clutch to keep the bag secure while out and about. Position the fasteners in place at approx. mid-centre against either lengthwise side of the folded edge of the clutch. Affix the stud part of the fastener to one side of the bag and the socket part of the fastener to the other side with a neat whipstitch using a hand-sewing needle and some matching thread. Trim off loose threads, fold in half, secure with the snapper and you're ready to go!

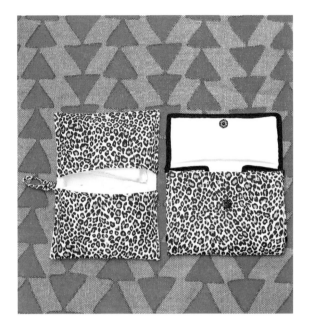

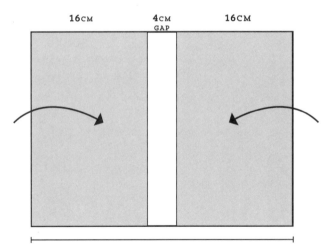

16CM   4CM GAP   16CM

36CM

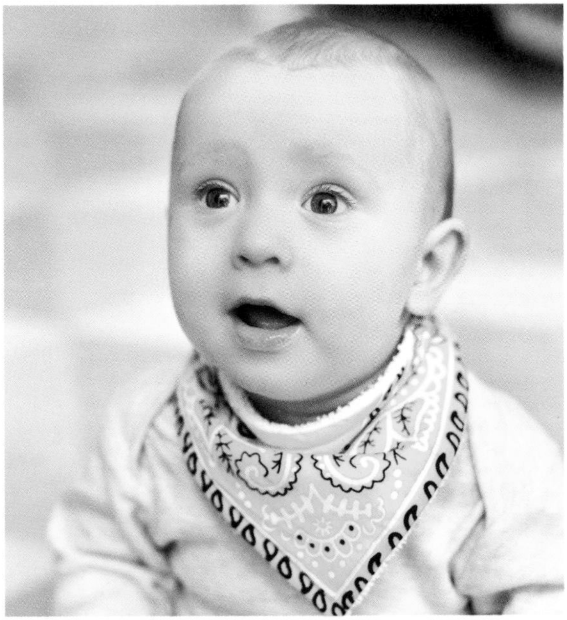
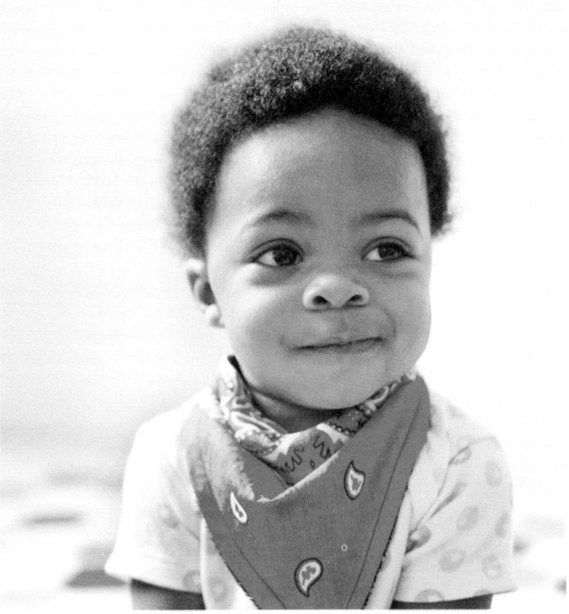
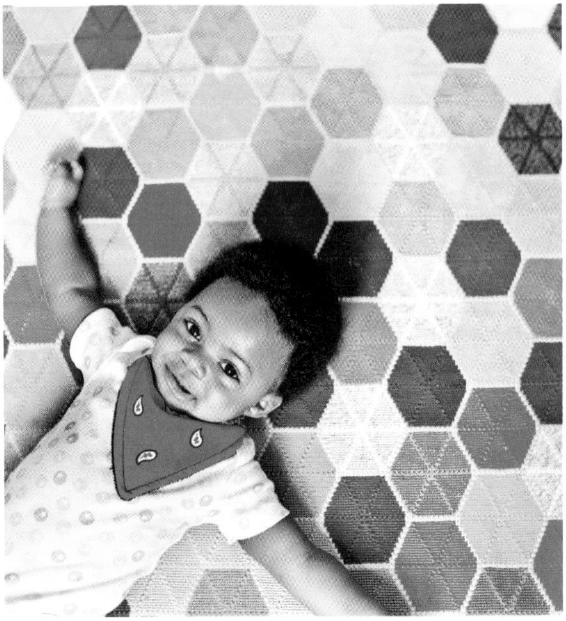
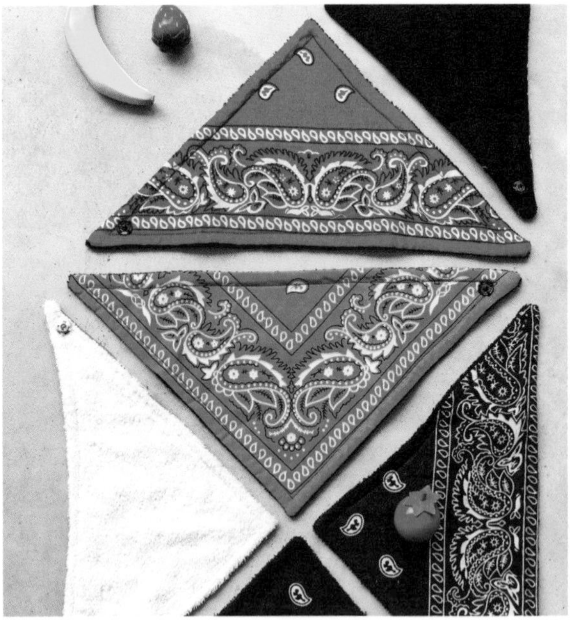

BANDANA BABY BIBS

Giddy-up! Calling all cowboys and cowgirls! Help keep your baby's threads pristine during messy mealtimes with one of these adorable and oh-so-easy to sew baby bandana bibs. These vintage-style neckerchiefs have the added bonus of being both practical and fun. With a nostalgic nod to the distinctive paisley print, I like to make mine up in a selection of bold, modern, bright colours. Bandanas not your style? Raid your fabric stash, pick out an assortment of cheerful cottons and whip them up to match any outfit.

HOW TO

1. Wash and press all your fabrics before getting started. Photocopy or trace the bib template on page 147, enlarging by the required percentage, onto paper or thin card. Cut out the template with paper scissors. Use the template to mark and then cut out both the bandana and towelling fabrics, aligning the straight edge with a fold in the fabrics as indicated on the template.

2. Pin both fabric pattern pieces together with right sides facing together, aligning all edges. Sew around the edges with a straight stitch, using a 1cm seam allowance and leaving a 2cm gap for turning the right sides out.

3. Clip the corners, then turn the right sides out. Be sure to poke the corners out to sharp points – use a pencil or a knitting needle to help you. Press to form neat edges.

4. Topstitch 0.5cm around the entire edge of the bib, catching the open seam to close it as you stitch along.

5. To finish, hand sew your snaps on approx. 1cm in from each top corner edge with a secure whipstitch. The 'innie' or socket part of the fastener should be attached to the back (towelling) side of the bib and the 'outie' or stud half of the fastener should be attached to the front right side of the bandana bib.

FINISHED SIZE

Approx. 18cm from top to bottom
x approx. 36cm from tip to tip,
for neck circumference
Suitable from birth

MATERIALS

Template (see page 147)
1 bandana or 25cm square of
printed cotton fabric, washed
and pressed
25cm square of lightweight
towelling fabric
Matching threads
1 pair of 13mm sew-on snap
fasteners

SUPPLIES

Paper or card for templates
Paper scissors
Fabric scissors
Pins
Sewing machine
Hand-sewing needle
Iron

STITCHES USED

Straight stitch
Whipstitch

TEMPLATES – see page 147

Bib

REVERSIBLE BABY BONNET

A simple two-piece reversible baby bonnet will finish off any outfit, and with its sweet retro feel it'll keep your baby's head cute and cosy for strolls in the park or out and about on the town. This bonnet has the added bonus of being one size fits all – simply cinch the ties to tighten the gathers at the back to adjust the size to fit your baby's head. I sometimes like to embellish these with a colourful, delicate trim but they also look cool kept simple for a modern minimal look. It's totally wearable for both girls or boys and a popular baby shower gift.

HOW TO CUT THE FABRIC

1. Photocopy or trace the bonnet hood and back templates on page 142, enlarging by the required percentage, onto paper or thin card. Cut out the templates with paper scissors. Arrange the templates on the outer fabric as shown on the fabric cutting guide on page 142.

2. Mark and cut one hood and back from the outer fabric, and then a second hood and back from the lining fabric. Cut out a strip of fabric for ties measuring 120cm x 3.5cm.

CONSTRUCT, PIN AND SEW

3. Pin the two hood pieces together with right sides facing, pin the hood around the back piece, with right sides facing together, easing it to fit as you go along. Sew together using a 1cm seam allowance. Trim down the seam allowance and zigzag along the seam edges to add extra reinforcement.

continued on the next page

SIZE

One size fits all
Suitable from birth

MATERIALS

Templates (see page 142)
0.25m soft cotton for bonnet
   outer (reversible if you are
   not making a lining)
0.25m soft co-ordinating cotton
   for lining
Matching threads
Trim (optional)

SUPPLIES

Paper or card for templates
Paper scissors
Fabric scissors
Tape measure
Fabric marker pen or tailor's chalk
Pins
Pinking shears
Sewing machine and/or
   hand-sewing needle
Iron
Oversized safety pin

STITCHES USED

Straight stitch
Zigzag stitch

TEMPLATES – see page 142

Bonnet hood and back

4. Now attach the lining to the outer fabric – place both pieces together with the wrong sides facing together and right sides of each fabric facing outwards. Match up the seam lines and align all edges, then pin together.

5. Fold down the raw edge of the hood to the underside of the bonnet by 0.5cm and then another 0.5cm to create a neat double-fold hem. Pin into place, then stitch as close to the outside edge of the hem as possible using a straight stitch. Turn this hem back over itself so it's sitting onto the front right side of the hood and pin into place. Stitch all the way along the opposite outside edge of the hem to create a second line of topstitching. This will add some extra stability to the hood. Press the bonnet neatly.

6. Next, move on to the open neck seam. Turn the seam under to the inside of the bonnet by 1cm and press. Turn under another 1cm, press again, then pin into place. This bottom hem will also become the casing for the gathering ties.

7. Sew the casing hem into place as close to the top edge as possible and leave both ends of the seam open, ready to insert the ties.

MAKE THE TIES

8. You can make the ties using either the leftover outer or lining fabric. Follow the method as the Dummy Ribbon Clips on page 84; the only difference is your tie will be much longer and not attached to a popper or clip at each end.

9. To attach the tie to the bonnet, pin an oversized safety pin onto one end of the fabric tie and guide it through the open bottom casing seam all the way through and out the other side. Knot the ends for a final flourish!

Keep it simple!
For a super easy make, forget the lining and choose a soft, reversible fabric. If you don't want the bother of making your own fabric ties you can use ribbon or bias tape.

FELT MOCCASINS

Stitch your little squaw a pair of handmade baby moccasins – a style-savvy choice for cool mamas everywhere and a personal footwear favourite of my own! These felt shoes are ideal for babies as they're soft and snug and easy to slip on and off. Plus they are a perfect project for using up any leftover felt scraps you might have in your stash. Try making them in contrasting colours, embellished with a little embroidery, ribbon or felt detailing. They can be sewn either by hand using a small neat whipstitch or on the machine using a mix of straight and zigzag stitches.

HOW TO CUT THE FABRIC

1. Photocopy or trace the required templates on page 144 onto paper or thin card. Cut out each template with paper scissors.

2. Cut out all the pattern pieces using the templates as follows:

    🐦 Sole – cut out four in felt, cut out two interfacing to add some stiffness and stability to the soles of the moccasins.

    🐦 Tongue – cut out two in felt

    🐦 Side – cut out two in felt

    🐦 Fringe – cut out two in contrasting felt

MAKE THE SOLES

3. Trim the interfacing soles down by 0.5cm all around. Place one of the interfacing soles in between two of the felt soles and pin into place. In matching thread, sew around the

continued on the next page

SIZES
0–6 months – 10cm sole length
6–12 months – 12.5cm sole length

STITCHES USED
Straight stitch
Zigzag stitch
Whipstitch

MATERIALS
Templates (see page 144)
Felt scraps (use high-quality craft felt)
Off-cuts of non-woven sew-in interfacing
Matching thread
1m cord for ties, cut in half to create 2 x 50cm ties
Embellishments (optional)

SUPPLIES
Paper or card for templates
Paper scissors
Fabric marker pen or tailor's chalk
Fabric scissors
Tape measure
Pins
Sewing machine and/or hand-sewing needle

TEMPLATES – see page 144
Sole, tongue, back, fringe

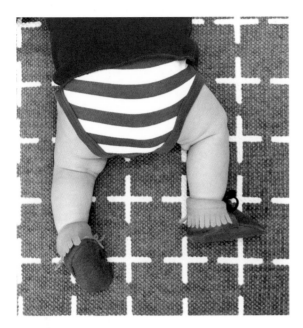

entire edge of the sole either on the machine using a small zigzag stitch or by hand with a small whipstitch. Repeat for the second shoe and then put both soles aside.

ASSEMBLE THE FRINGE AND BACK PANEL

4. Attach the fringe section to the back piece to create a back panel fringe. To do so, place the back panel, right side up, on a flat surface then place the fringe panel right side up on top of the heel, with both top edges sitting flush against each other. Pin into place, then sew along this top seam using a 0.5cm seam allowance. Flip the fringe panel over the top of

the seam you have just sewn, so that it is sitting on top of and slightly above the back panel to create a fold.

5. Place one lace cord in the fold at the top of the back panel so that it is resting against the seam line and pin it into place. Stitch 1cm in from the top of the folded edge, across the width of the fringe panel to create a casing to keep the cord tie in place. Now shape and trim the fringe piece by making a series of snips into the panel to create a fringed effect. Be careful not to cut too close to the stitching.

continued on the next page

ATTACH THE BACK PANEL TO THE SOLE

6. To assemble the shoe, begin by attaching the fringed back panel to the sole with right sides together. Pin and ease into place around the back of the sole making sure not to catch any of the fringe as you do.

7. Stitch into place using either a zigzag stitch or whipstitch and backstitch at either end for extra strength. Repeat for the other shoe, and leave inside out for the next stage.

EMBELLISH AND ATTACH THE TONGUES

8. Before attaching the tongue to the sole, stitch on your chosen embellishment to the front centre of each right side of the tongue pieces. Do this for each shoe.

9. To finish assembling the shoe you will need to stitch the tongue to the front of the sole. Pin the tongue with the right side facing against the front rounded toe end of the sole, easing it into place as you pin. Each side of the tongue should overlap on top of the fringed back panel once stitched into place, so that when the shoe is turned right sides out the tongue will be resting on the inside, with the back panel sitting on the outside of shoe.

10. Stitch the sole and tongue together with a zigzag stitch or whipstitch. Do this for each shoe.

11. Turn the tongue and the fringed back panel right side out so the visible stitching is on the inside of the shoe. Smooth out the seam lines by finger-pressing the felt into shape for a neat finish.

DUMMY RIBBON CLIPS

Never lose another dummy! My daughter was always throwing hers out of the pram so these were a personal must-have during her early days of babyhood. You can find plastic clips online, or try a good department store or haberdashery for metal mitten or suspender clips. Then style up your your own customised dummy clips made from your favourite fabrics or ribbons. The ultimate on-the-go accessory, they even double up as buggy clips, useful for attaching toys and all sorts of other pushchair paraphernalia. Remember to keep the ribbons to standard size for baby-safe style.

HOW TO

1. Take the fabric strip and fold it in half lengthwise with wrong sides facing together, and press.

2. Unfold the strip, then fold under the two short ends, with wrong sides together, by 0.5cm and press.

3. Bring the two long sides inwards to meet at the centre crease and press to create two long folded fabric edges.

4. Fold the strip in half lengthwise along the crease made in step 1 and press into place.

5. To secure, use a straight stitch to hand- or machine-sew all the way around the entire ribbon strip as close to the outside edges as possible. Trim off any loose threads.

6. Guide one end of the fabric strip through the clip opening. Fold the end down by 2cm and stitch firmly into place.

7. To keep the dummy handle attached to the ribbon clip, make a fold in the free end of the fabric ribbon 6cm from the end, bringing the end up towards the clip. Attach your pieces of hook and loop fastening or snap poppers in the centre of the ribbon on corresponding sides, approx. 1cm in from the free end, and you're done!

SIZE
22cm long (standard size for safety)

MATERIALS
10 x 36cm cotton fabric strip
Matching thread
Clip
Small piece of hook and loop
  fastening, or snap popper

SUPPLIES
Tape measure
Fabric marker pen or tailor's chalk
Fabric scissors
Sewing machine and/or
  hand-sewing needle
Iron

STITCHES USED
Straight stitch

BABY'S BEST BLOOMERS

Handmade baby bloomers will dress up a dull nappy and look great either worn under little dresses for girls or slung on with a cool tee for boys. My daughter even wears these in winter over a pair of cosy tights. Pick out a selection of soft, comfortable cottons in pretty patterns and stitch up a pair for every day of the week! This project requires just a little easy pattern pinning – see the fabric cutting guide (see page 146) for cutting out directions, taking note of the seam placements within the pattern.

HOW TO CUT THE FABRIC

1. Photocopy or trace the bloomers front and back templates on page 146, enlarging by the required percentage, onto paper or thin card. Cut out the templates with paper scissors.

2. Follow the fabric cutting guide on page 146 for pattern placement on your fabric. Fold the fabric together as indicated by bringing the two selvedges in to meet at the middle.

3. Place both the front and back bloomer templates against the folded edges of the fabric and pin into place, then cut out. Use either tailor's chalk or a water-soluble fabric pen to transfer markings from the pattern pieces onto the wrong side of your fabric pieces, including front, back and the seam placements for reference. This will help you match the seams for the next step – sewing up!

continued on the next page

SIZES
0–6 months
6–12 months

MATERIALS
Templates (see page 146)
0.5m pre-shrunk cotton for bloomers, waist and legband casings
Matching threads
1cm width elastic –
    90cm for 0–6 months
    105cm for 6–12 months

SUPPLIES
Paper or card for templates
Paper scissors
Pins
Fabric scissors
Fabric marker pen or tailor's chalk
Sewing machine
Tape measure
Iron
Oversized safety pin

STITCHES USED
Straight stitch
Zigzag stitch

TEMPLATES – see page 146
Bloomers front and back
Note which are the Side Seam (SS) and Crotch Seam (CS) as this will help when you stitch the two pieces together.

SEW THE FABRIC PIECES TOGETHER

4. Unpin and unfold the front and back pieces, placing them on top of each other with right sides together and with the side seams (SS) aligned. Sew the side seams together using a straight stitch and 1cm seam allowance.

5. Trim the seam allowance. To add some extra reinforcement and finish off the seams, sew along the raw edges with a small zigzag stitch.

6. Next, join the front and the back crotch seams (CS), stitching right sides together with a straight stitch and 1cm seam allowance. Trim and reinforce the seam with a zigzag stitch as for the side seams.

MAKE AN ELASTICATED WAISTBAND

7. To create an elasticated waistband you need to make a fabric casing to enclose the elastic, which will be added separately to the bloomers. To do this, measure the circumference of the bloomers' waist to get the length of the casing strip and add 1cm for 0.5cm seam allowance at either end. Cut a strip of matching fabric using this measurement as the length, and 5cm wide.

8. Turn one of the longest edges of the casing strip under by 1cm towards the wrong side of the fabric and press. With right sides of the fabric facing together, bring the two short ends of the casing strip together and join using 0.5cm seam allowance to create one piece of casing. Trim the seam allowance.

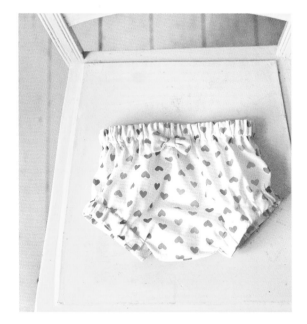

9. Pin the unpressed side of the casing strip around the raw waistband edge of the bloomers with right sides facing and stitch together using a 0.5cm seam allowance.

10. Press the stitched edge of the casing under towards the inside of the bloomers to create a top folded seam line. The casing should not be visible from the bloomers' right side. Pin into place, then topstitch 0.5cm in from the folded edge of the casing, leaving a 3cm gap open for inserting the elastic.

11. Cut 40cm (smaller size) or 45cm (larger size) from the piece of elastic for the waistband and attach the oversized safety pin to one end. Poke it through the gap in the open seam and thread it through the casing, guiding it all the way around the waistband and out at the other side

of the opening, being careful not to twist it as you do. This will create an elasticated gathered waist.

12. Pull both ends of the elastic out of the casing, overlap them by 1cm and sew together using a zigzag stitch. To be extra secure I like to backstitch a few times over this seam.

13. Once the waistband is secure, close the gap in the casing by following the topstitching line, either on a sewing machine or by hand, making sure not to catch the elastic as you sew. Backstitch at either end of the stitching to secure.

continued on the next page

MAKE ELASTICATED LEG BANDS

14. You will also need to create elasticated leg
    bands to finish each of the leg openings.
    Measure the circumference of the leg openings
    and add 1cm for seam allowance. Cut two strips
    of matching fabric for the leg band casings
    using this measurement as the length, and 5cm
    as the width.

15. Prepare and stitch the leg bands as for the
    waistband (steps 8–13), leaving a 2cm opening
    in the casing for inserting the elastic, and
    cutting two pieces of elastic at either 25cm
    (0–6 months) or 30cm (6–12 months).

EMBELLISH

16. Make mini baby bows to embellish your
    bloomers! See the Hair Bows page 96 for the
    baby bow instructions and stitch into place
    either onto the front of the waistband or on
    each side of the leg bands.

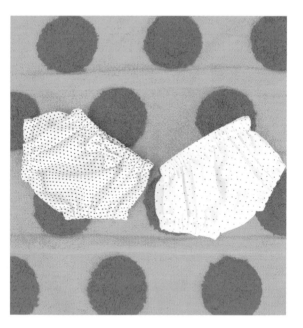

BABY DUNGAREES

Dungarees are a classic childhood style staple and a personal favourite of mine and my daughter's. Not only do they suit both boys and girls, but they also offer a practical solution to keeping crawling knees covered as your baby begins to explore the world around them. You can can make your own pair of dungarees with some soft but sturdy denim or a cute cotton twill. Do remember to pre-shrink and press all fabric before using.

HOW TO CUT THE FABRIC

1. Photocopy or trace the dungarees front body, back body, dungarees front facing and back facing templates on page 157, enlarging by the required percentage, onto paper or thin card. Cut out the templates with paper scissors.

2. Fold the fabric in half, selvedge to selvedge, to cut out all the pieces on double thickness fabric. Using the templates, pin, mark and cut out a pair of the dungarees front body and a pair of the back body from the denim fabric, and a a pair of front facing and a pair of back facing from the cotton fabric, using the layout diagram (see page 159) as a guide.

3. Mark the notches on the fabric pieces by snipping into the seam allowances to help you match up the seams.

JOIN THE PIECES TOGETHER

4. Zigzag the front body CF seams down to the crotch on both pieces. Place the two front body pieces together with right sides of the fabric facing and edges aligned. Sew

continued on the next page

SIZES

0–6 months
6–12 months

MATERIALS

Templates (see page 157)
1m lightweight soft denim
  or cotton twill
0.25m soft cotton print
  fabric for facing
Matching threads
2 pairs of 18mm sew-on
  snap fasteners

SUPPLIES

Paper or card for templates
Paper scissors
Pins
Fabric marker pen or tailor's chalk
Fabric scissors
Sewing machine and/or
  hand-sewing needle
Iron

STITCHES USED

Straight stitch
Zigzag stitch
Slipstitch

TEMPLATES – see page 157

Dungarees front body, back body,
  front facing, back facing

the CF seams together all the way down to the crotch using a straight stitch and a 1cm seam allowance. Press the seams open.

5. Place the two front facing pieces together with right sides facing inwards. Stitch the CF seams together using a straight stitch and a 1cm seam allowance. Turn the bottom seam under by 1cm towards the wrong side of the fabric and topstitch into place.

6. Repeat step 4 for both the back body pieces, stitching along the CB seam all the way down to the crotch. Press the seams open.

7. Repeat step 5 for the back body pieces, stitching along the CB seam. Turn under the bottom seam on CB facing and topstitch into place.

ATTACH FACING TO DUNGAREES

8. With right sides of the fabric together, align the front body and front facing and stitch together around the armhole, strap and front neck. Trim down the seam allowance and clip approx. 2–4mm around all curves. Turn right sides out. Open the armhole seams out flat and topstitch around the armhole curve on top of the facing, approx. 2mm in from the seam edge, for approx. 8cm. Repeat around the front neck hole, topstitching approx. 2mm in from the seam edge on top of the facing.

9. Repeat step 8 for the back body and back facing, topstitching the facing around the armholes and neck as before.

JOIN THE FRONT, BACK AND LEGS

10. Align the front and back body pieces, right sides facing. Bring the back facing over so that the front body and back body facings are now aligned and facing together, with right sides of the fabric on top of each other. Pin the side seams of the back and front body together and stitch using a zigzag stitch and a 1cm seam allowance to prevent fraying. Repeat for the other leg and turn right sides out.

11. Sew the inner leg seams together using a zigzag stitch, then use a straight stitch to join them together from front to back, following the arc of the inside leg seam.

FINISHING TOUCHES

12. Neaten the lower edges of the trouser seams with a double-turned hem. Simply fold the fabric under towards the wrong side by 0.5cm and press. Fold again by 1cm, press and stitch into place as close to the folded edge as possible.

13. To secure the dungarees at the straps, position and stitch on a pair of sew-on snap fasteners at each end of both of the straps. Try the dungarees on the wearer beforehand, if you can, to get the correct placement.

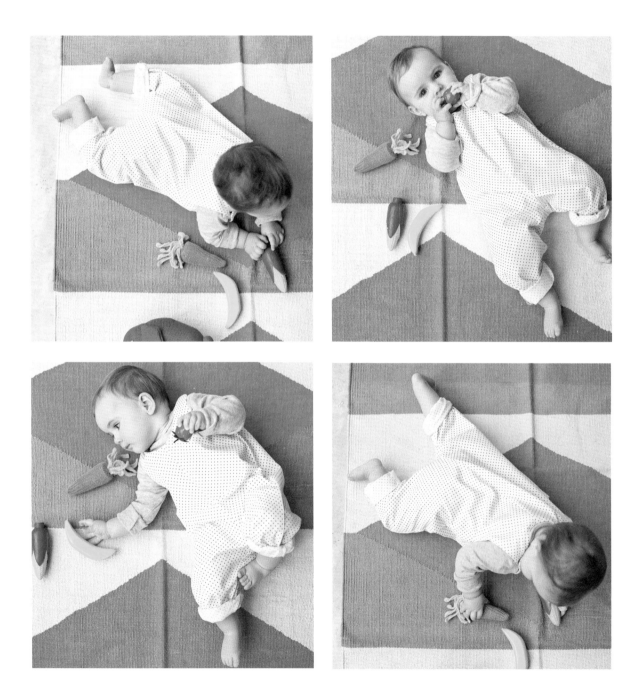

HAIR BOWS

To make a bow for a little girl's hair, pick out a selection of pretty cotton fabric scraps to match her outfits, then stitch up and style! These bows also look super-sweet stitched onto the front of onesies, or used to decorate the baby bloomers on pages 86–91.

HOW TO

1. Cut your fabric to the correct size. To make a small bow (0–6 months), cut out a large fabric rectangle measuring 13 x 8cm. Cut another smaller rectangle measuring 5 x 2.5cm – this is for the middle strip to finish the bow. To make a larger bow (6–12 months), cut out a fabric rectangle measuring 15 x 10cm. Cut another smaller rectangle measuring 5 x 2.5cm.

2. Fold the larger fabric rectangle in half lengthwise with right sides together. Pin and then stitch along the long edge with a 0.5cm seam allowance to create a fabric tube.

3. Turn the right sides out and press with the seam in the middle of the tube. Fold the two short open ends over to the back (seam side) of the fabric tube so that they meet in the middle, overlapping slightly.

4. Stitch the folded ends into place by sewing a straight line along the midpoint of the rectangle, then gather and pinch the middle to create the bow shape and secure in position with a few hand stitches.

5. Now you have your basic bow you will need to neaten and finish the front with the smaller rectangle of fabric. Fold the two long raw edges under to the meet in the middle of the wrong side of the fabric and press. Wrap this strip around the middle of the bow and fold towards the back, securing with some neat stitches.

6. Fix your bow onto a baby-safe alligator clip, either with some neat hand stitches or a few dabs of hot glue.

SIZES
0–6 months
6–12 months

MATERIALS
2 cotton fabric scraps, at least 15 x 10cm and 5 x 2.5cm (these will make the smaller bow)
Matching thread
Baby-safe alligator hair clip

SUPPLIES
Tape measure
Fabric scissors
Pins
Sewing machine
Hand-sewing needle
Iron

STITCHES USED
Straight stitch

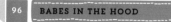

BABY BOW TIES

Make a baby boy a bow tie to stitch onto onesies or attach to a clip to wear with a shirt for a real dapper chap! If you don't want to use a clip or attach the bow permanently you can either stitch the bow to some elastic to create an easy pull on and off version, or you can get really fancy and make a proper necktie with some leftover matching fabric – an irresistible accompaniment to baby onesies complete with real shirt collars, which are now widely available.

HOW TO

1. Take the larger fabric rectangle and fold it in half lengthwise, with right sides together. Pin and sew along the long edge with a 0.5cm seam allowance to create a fabric tube.

2. Turn the right side out and press with the seam in the middle of the tube. Fold the two short open ends over to the back (seam side) of the fabric tube so that they meet in the middle, overlapping slightly. This will become the back of the bow. Pinch and gather the middle of the bow, securing with a few stitches to keep its shape.

3. Take the smaller fabric rectangle for the middle piece and fold the two shorter edges in to the centre, with wrong sides together. Press. If you are making a simple bow tie to sew onto a onesie, wrap this middle strip around the necktie, fold towards the back and stitch into place neatly to finish. Then attach your bow tie to the onesie of your choice.

continued on the next page

SIZE
6–12 months

MATERIALS
2 cotton fabric scraps 21 x 16cm
   and 6 x 7cm
Matching thread
Soft elastic for pull-on elasticated
   pull-on bow tie (optional)
Cotton fabric scrap for proper
   fabric bow tie, at least
   35 x 7cm (optional)
1cm piece of hook and loop
   fastening for necktie (optional)

SUPPLIES
Sewing machine
Hand-sewing needle
Fabric scissors
Pins
Iron

STITCHES USED
Straight stitch

FOR ELASTICATED PULL-ON BOW TIE

4. Put the pressed fabric for the middle strip to one side. Measure the circumference of the baby's neck, being careful not to measure too tightly. You should be able to slip two fingers between the tape measure and the baby's neck easily.

5. Cut a length of elastic 2cm longer than the baby's neck circumference. Stitch the ends securely together, overlapping by 1cm. Hold the bow tie against the join, wrap the middle strip around the elastic and the centre of the bow, fold towards the back and stitch into place neatly to finish.

FOR PROPER FABRIC BOW TIE

6. Put the pressed fabric for the middle strip to one side. Measure the circumference of the baby's neck, being careful not to measure too tightly. You should be able to slip two fingers between the tape measure and the baby's neck easily.

7. Cut a strip of fabric 7cm wide and 4cm longer than the baby's neck circumference. Turn under the two short edges of the strip to the wrong side of the fabric by 1cm and press. Fold the strip in half lengthwise, wrong sides together, and press again. Unfold this central crease and bring the two long edges in to meet at the crease, with wrong sides together. Press. Fold in half along the central crease and press once more.

8. Before stitching the neck strap you will need to attach the hook and loop fastening in place to create a seamless look. Pull the piece of fastening apart. Position one part at one end of the strap and the other part at the opposite end. Unfold the strap and stitch each piece into place approx. 0.5cm in from the edge, making sure to catch only one layer of fabric as you sew.

9. Stitch along the open folded edge of the neck strap strip using a straight stitch as close to the edge as possible. Place the bow against the centre of the neck strap, wrap the middle strip around the neck strap and the centre of the bow, fold towards the back and stitch into place neatly to finish.

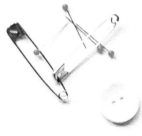

BABES IN TOYLAND
PLAYTIME FOR BABY

Babies progress at such a rapid pace that keeping up-to-date with their developing skills can mean providing them with an ever-increasing stack of toys, which can become expensive. But if you can bring your creative skills into play and have a go at making your own then you'll not only have loads of fun but will also save yourself some pennies. Plus what's more satisfying than seeing your little one enjoying your own homemade handiwork?

Interactive playtime is essential for babies as not only does it boost bonding time but it also helps stimulate development. Hours of fun can be spent making playthings using soft textures, bold patterns and high contrast colours – try stitching a set of building blocks or stacking rings and pair up with a patchwork playmat for the ultimate playtime set. Or grab your baby's attention with a homemade rattle or a playful pram toy!

ANIMAL RATTLES

Babies love to explore faces and expressions and these cute animal rattles will not fail to capture their attention! My daughter loved learning to recognise and name her favourite creatures as not only do these rattles help to focus attention, they're perfect for little hands to grip and help stimulate a baby's sense of sound as they learn to rattle and shake. This set of three includes a fox, an owl and a panda bear – take a walk on the wild side and make these for the baby in your life!

HOW TO MAKE THE FOX RATTLE

1. Photocopy or trace the fox and fox appliqué templates on page 139 onto paper or thin card. Cut out the templates with paper scissors.

2. Use the fox template to mark and cut out two shapes (for the front and back) from orange cotton fabric scraps or the coloured cotton of your choice.

3. Use the fox appliqué templates to mark and cut out all the facial details from a variety of coloured felt scraps – use the photo on page 107 as a guide.

4. Build up the appliqué face with your felt pieces. Lay one of the fox face shapes, right side up, on a flat surface. Start with the Fox eyes – stitch the two eye components together and into position on the fabric on top of the two cheeks. Use a straight stitch or a zigzag stitch for the appliqué. Position the two cheek appliqués approx. 1cm in from the edge of the fabric shape and stitch down. Stitch the two ear appliqués into place approx. 2cm in from the edges.

5. Now the appliqué face has been sewn you can sew the two fox pieces together. Pin the pieces with right sides facing

SIZE
13 x 13cm

MATERIALS
Templates (see pages 138–140)
Fabric scraps – less than 0.25m
    per rattle
Felt scraps for appliqué details
Matching threads
Rattle insert (optional)
Polyester toy stuffing

SUPPLIES
Paper or card for templates
Paper scissors
Fabric marker pen or tailor's chalk
Fabric scissors
Sewing machine and/or
    hand-sewing needle
Pins

STITCHES USED
Straight Stitch
Zigzag stitch
Whipstitch

TEMPLATES – see pages
    138–140
Fox, fox appliqué, owl,
    owl appliqué, panda,
    panda appliqué

continued on the next Page

together with all edges aligned. Sew around the outline using a 1cm seam allowance. When you get to the cheeks you want to make sure your line of stitching sits just outside and around the edge of the appliqué rather than on top of it. Leave a 3cm gap for turning between the ears.

6. Trim down the seam allowance to 6mm and clip any curved corners. Remember – be careful not to snip into the seam as you do. Turn the right side out, smoothing the seam into place with your fingers and poking the ears and the nose into shape.

7. Press with an iron on the back in order to not distort the felt. Stuff with polyester toy stuffing until the fox is nice and firm. Add your rattle insert, if using, and stitch the open seam closed with a neat whipstitch.

FOR THE OWL RATTLE

8. Follow the same method as the fox rattle, using the owl and owl appliqué templates. For the appliqué, stitch the eye components together and then onto the fabric. Stitch the chest triangles onto the chest appliqué before stitching the chest appliqué to the fabric 1cm in from the bottom of the fabric. Stitch the beak on last, slightly overlapping onto the chest.

FOR THE PANDA RATTLE

9. Follow the same method as for the fox rattle, using the panda and panda appliqué templates. For the appliqué, stitch the three eye components together and then onto the fabric. Stitch the nose into place below the eyes, and

the mouth just below the nose, approx. 1.5cm in from the side edges. Finally, stitch the ear pieces into position 1cm in from the edge of the fabric.

You can find inexpensive rattle inserts online – try eBay!

BABY'S FIRST FLASH CARDS

Make learning fun with a deck of DIY flash cards to help your baby memorise numbers, letters, shapes and colours. I made mine using a mixture of bold shapes and brightly coloured numbers but, if you're skilled with a pen, why not draw your own pictures and graphics to create a custom-made deck. Stitch the cards two-sided so you can flip them over to reveal a different shape or number. And remember, flash cards aren't just for learning but also look great displayed around the nursery as DIY decoration.

HOW TO

1. Measure out a flash card template with a ruler onto paper or thin card. Photocopy or trace the number and shape templates on pages 154–155 onto paper or thin card. Cut out the templates with paper scissors.

2. Using the flash card template, mark and cut out two felt rectangles. If you decide to make your cards double-sided choose different colours for each side to add more interest. Again, using the template, mark and cut one rectangle of interfacing, then trim it down by 0.5cm on all sides.

3. Choose your first design template – numbers or shapes. Mark and cut out the shape in contrasting-coloured felt ready for stitching. Position the cut-out shape on the front centre of the felt rectangle. Pin into place and stitch down either using a zigzag, straight or satin stitch on a sewing machine or whipstitch or blanket stitch by hand.

4. Once the appliqué has been sewn, sandwich the interfacing between the two felt rectangles, with the appliqué side facing outwards. Stitch the layers together by sewing around the outside edge using a zigzag stitch on the machine or a blanket stitch by hand. Trim off any loose threads and repeat with each of the number and shape templates for a complete set of cards.

FINISHED SIZE
9 x 13cm
Suitable from birth

MATERIALS
Templates (see pages 154–155)
18 rectangles of felt each
    measuring 9 x 13cm
9 rectangles of interfacing
    measuring 9 x 13cm
Felt scraps for appliqué
Matching threads

SUPPLIES
Ruler
Paper or card for templates
Paper scissors
Fabric marker pen or tailor's chalk
Fabric scissors
Pins
Sewing machine and/or
    hand-sewing needle

STITCHES USED
Straight stitch
Zigzag or satin stitch
    (if sewing by machine)
Whipstitch or blanket stitch
    (if sewing by hand)

TEMPLATES – see pages
    154–155
Numbers and shapes

BABY GARLAND

A colourful garland is a multipurpose piece of baby kit as it can be used to hang beside the crib or above the pram and even tied to a car seat to keep your baby entertained on the go. It can also double up as nursery bunting for a super-stylish and bold wall decoration. My geometric garland does require quite a bit of careful cutting out but it will be well worth it for the finished 3D effect. It also has the added bonus of being totally customisable as you can make it as long or as short as you like using any number of the prism shapes of your choice.

HOW TO CUT THE FABRIC

1. Photocopy or trace the garland shape and garland backing templates on page 143, enlarging by the required percentage, onto paper or thin card. Cut out the templates with paper scissors.

2. Using the backing templates, mark and cut out two of each shape in your chosen backing felt colour – I used black felt for a high contrast look.

3. Using the appliqué templates mark and cut out the appliqué pieces for each of the garland shapes in a variety of coloured felt to create the geometric appliqué. Use the photo on pages 112–113 as a guide. The trick to working with felt is to be very precise with your cutting out – I prefer to use a rotary cutter, cutting mat and transparent ruler for cutting angles and straight edges, but as long as you're steady with a pair of scissors cutting the fabric should not be a problem.

continued on the next page

FINISHED SIZE
1m
Suitable from birth

MATERIALS
Templates (see page 143)
0.25m felt for backing fabric
Felt scraps in an assortment
   of colours
Matching threads
1m bias tape, double-fold
   bias binding or ribbon

SUPPLIES
Paper or card for templates
Paper scissors
Fabric marker pen or tailor's chalk
Rotary cutter, cutting mat and
   ruler or fabric scissors
Fabric glue (optional)
Sewing machine and/or
   hand-sewing needle
Pins

STITCHES USED
Straight stitch
Zigzag stitch (optional)
Whipstitch (if hand sewing)

TEMPLATES – see page 143
Garland shape and garland
   backing appliqué

ASSEMBLE AND SEW THE SHAPES

4. Assemble the coloured cut-out shapes onto one
    of the corresponding backing template shapes
    – again, use the photo above as a guide. Try to
    keep the spacing between the cut-out shapes
    as even and equal as possible – approx. 3mm.
    You may want to stick the shapes down with
    some fabric glue before securing with stitching.
    If using glue, leave to dry before sewing the
    shape cut-outs into place. To do this, use
    matching threads and straight or zigzag stitch
    on the sewing machine, or, if sewing by hand,
    use a neat whipstitch. Trim off all loose threads
    for a neat finish.

5. Take the second backing shape and place this
    against the back of your built up design to
    cover up and finish the raw stitching. Align
    the two fabric shapes and pin. Sew the shapes
    together around the edge of the border using a
    straight stitch and some matching thread.

6. Repeat steps 4 and 5 for the other shapes,
    taking care with spacing the coloured felt
    shapes and ensuring you use matching
    coloured threads. I used seven prism shapes
    spaced approx. 15cm apart for my 1m garland.

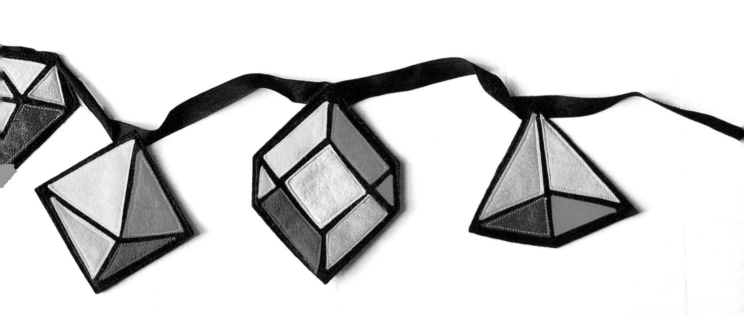

ATTACH SHAPES TO THE RIBBON

7. To hang your shapes you can create a garland using bias tape, double-fold bias binding or ribbon. Cut the length of your binding to the preferred size depending on how many shapes you want to hang. If using double-fold bias binding, stitch the fold closed first.

8. Fold both ends of the binding back to create loops for hanging and stitch into place. Fix your shapes onto the front of the binding and secureinto place with a line of stitching against the top border of the felt using matching thread for a seamless effect.

SOFT STACKING RINGS

Most shop-bought stacking toys are made from either plastic or wood, so this set is an unusual soft handmade take on this baby play essential. Stacking rings are a key developmental toy as they can help strengthen babies' hand-eye co-ordination, so be adventurous with your choice of fabric colour and pattern and create an eye-catching toy that babies will love to look at as well as touch. Embellish with some ribbons securely sewn into the seams for a little bit more fun and flair!

HOW TO CUT THE FABRIC

1. Photocopy or trace the templates on page 156, enlarging by the required percentage, onto paper or thin card. Cut out each template with paper scissors. Cut out all the pattern pieces from your templates in your chosen fabrics, following template instructions for placing on the fold of the fabric. Also, cut a side strip panel for the base that is 71 x 4cm – this includes an extra 1cm on all sides for the seam allowance.

MAKE THE BASE

2. Sew the two short edges of the base side strip right sides together using a 1cm seam allowance to create one circular strip. Press the seam open.

3. Pin the strip around the circumference of one of the base fabric circles with right sides together and sew all the way around using a 1cm seam allowance. Next, pin the other base fabric circle onto the opposite side of the side panel with right sides together and sew as before, but leave a 2cm gap for stuffing.

continued on the next page

FINISHED SIZE
Approx. 23 x 21cm
Suitable from birth

MATERIALS
Templates (see page 156)
Quilting-weight cotton fabric scraps
Matching threads
Polyester toy stuffing

SUPPLIES
Paper or card for templates
Paper scissors
Fabric marker pen or tailor's chalk
Fabric scissors
Tape measure
Sewing machine and/or
    hand-sewing needle
Iron
Pins

STITCHES USED
Straight stitch
Zigzag stitch
Whipstitch

TEMPLATES – see page 156
Stacking ring base, cylinder body
    and top, four stacking rings

4. Clip notches into the seams to help minimise bulk – space the notches approx. 1cm apart, then turn the right sides out. Fill the base with polyester toy stuffing until nice and firm, then sew the gap closed with small, neat whipstitches.

ASSEMBLE THE STACKING TUBE

5. Hem one of the short edges of the cylinder body by turning the raw edge under 0.5cm onto the wrong side of the fabric. Press, then stitch into place using a straight stitch as close to the seam edge as possible.

6. Next, fold the cylinder body in half with right sides of the fabric together, pin and sew up the long side seam using a scant 0.5cm seam allowance to create the cylinder tube.

7. With right sides together, pin the cylinder top circle to the raw open seam side of the cylinder tube. Stitch into place carefully using a scant 0.5cm seam. Turn right sides out and stuff firmly with polyester toy stuffing. Sew the stacking ring cylinder onto the top middle centre of the base with a secure whipstitch.

MAKE THE STACKING RINGS

8. Begin with your biggest ring first, using the two doughnut shapes cut from the ring one template. Also, cut a side panel strip measuring 71 x 4cm.

9. Sew the two short edges of the panel strip right sides together using a 1cm seam allowance to create one circular strip. Press the seam open.

With right sides together, pin the strip around the circumference of one of the fabric circles and sew all the way around using a 1cm seam allowance. Clip notches into the seam allowance, spacing the notches approx. 1cm apart.

10. Next, pin the other fabric circle onto the opposite side of the panel strip with right sides together and sew as before, leaving a 2cm gap for stuffing. Turn the right sides out.

11. To close up the ring you will need to sew the inner circle seam shut. Tuck the raw edges of the fabric under by 1cm and then stitch together, either by hand using a whipstitch or on the machine with a small zigzag stitch.

12. Stuff the ring with polyester toy stuffing using the 2cm gap at the side, filling just enough for the ring to hold its shape. Sew the gap closed with whipstitch.

13. Repeat steps 8–12 for the remaining rings, cutting side panel strips as follows:
    - Ring two 63 x 4cm
    - Ring three 55 x 4cm
    - Ring four 47.5 x 4cm

14. Stack the rings onto your ring base and play!

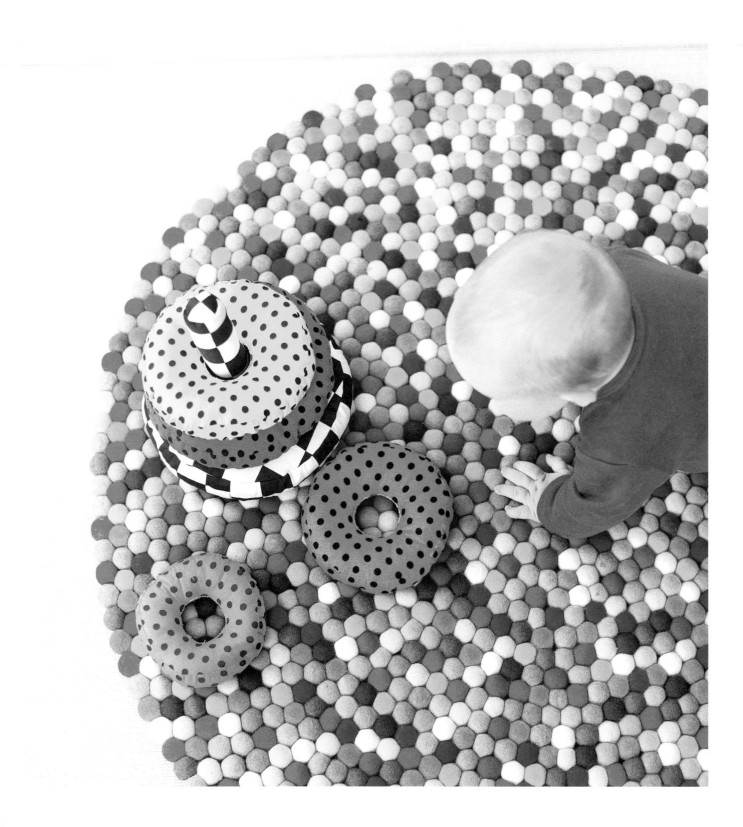

BABY BOOK

Stitching your own soft-play baby book is not only easy but also fun for baby and mum, too! Use bright, high-contrast colours and bold, eye-catching graphics to help kick-start baby's visual recognition of colours and shapes. Gather together an assortment of your favourite fabrics and, using the templates provided, stitch an action-packed 12-page whimsical weatherscape of colourful clouds, bright lightning bolts and eye-catching comets and stars to create a handmade treasure for your baby to love for many years to come.

HOW TO CUT OUT ALL PIECES

1. Photocopy or trace the graphics templates on page 153, enlarging by the required percentage, onto paper or thin card. Cut out the templates with paper scissors.

2. Using the book cover diagram on page 123 as a guide, mark and cut out two fabric rectangles for the front and back pages, plus one rectangle of wadding.

3. Using the inside pages diagram on page 123 as a guide, mark and cut out four fabric rectangles for the middle pages, plus two rectangles of wadding.

4. Use the graphics templates to mark and cut out all the graphics in an assortment of coloured felts – use the photos on pages 118, 121 and 122 as a guide.

MAKE THE FOLD OVER TAB CLOSURE

5. Measure, mark and cut out two fabric rectangles measuring 10 x 5cm for the fold-over tab closure.

6. Stitch the hook side of the hook and loop fastening to one of the shorter widthwise ends of the fabric rectangles – centre it onto the right side of the fabric, approx. 1.5cm in from the edge, and secure with a zigzag or straight stitch.

FINISHED SIZE
18 x 18cm

MATERIALS
Templates (see page 153)
2 rectangles of cotton fabric for book cover measuring 38cm x 20cm
4 rectangles of cotton fabric for inside book pages measuring 37cm x 19cm
Low-loft, lightweight wadding, 1 rectangle measuring 38cm x 20cm, plus 2 rectangles measuring 37cm x 19cm
Assortment of felt scraps for appliqué
1 rectangle of cotton fabric for fold-over tab closure measuring 20 x 10cm
Matching threads
3cm piece of hook and loop fastening

SUPPLIES
Paper or card for templates
Paper scissors
Fabric marker pen or tailor's chalk
Fabric scissors
Tape measure
Pins

...supplies, stitches and templates on the next page

continued on the next page

7. Align the two fabric rectangles with right sides together (hook fastening facing in) and pin together. Stitch around the edges with a 1cm seam allowance, leaving the opposite end to the fastening side open. Clip the corners and trim down excess seam allowance. Turn the right sides out and press. Set aside.

ASSEMBLE, APPLIQUÉ AND STITCH THE COVER AND INSIDE PAGES

8. Each fabric rectangle will become two pages divided by a stitched spine down the middle. So keep this layout in mind as you assemble the cut-out felt graphics onto the front centre of the cover, inside cover and each page. Use my the photos on pages 118, 121 and 122 as a guide. Remember when doing appliqué work to stitch securely as little babies will put anything and everything into their mouths!

9. Start with the cover and inside cover pages – these are formed from the two larger fabric rectangles. Assemble and pin the felt cut-outs in place, leaving 2cm around all edges to allow for seam allowance and topstitching. Sew them into place either on the machine with a zigzag or straight stitch, or by hand using a blanket or whipstitch. Stitch the soft loop side of the hook and loop fastening onto the front cover halfway down the right-hand side and 2cm in from the edge.

10. Stitch the cover and inside cover pages together – align the fabric rectangles with the right sides facing. Align the larger rectangle of

Sewing machine and/or hand-sewing needle
Iron

STITCHES USED
Straight stitch (if sewing by machine)
Zigzag stitch (optional)
Whipstitch (if sewing by hand)
Blanket stitch (optional)

TEMPLATES – see page 153
Graphics

wadding behind the two fabric rectangles and pin all three layers into place. Stitch the three layers together using a 1cm seam allowance around all sides, leaving a 6cm gap along the widthwise side of the back page (the opposite side to the hook and loop fastening end) for turning the right sides out and inserting the fold over tab closure. Trim off any loose threads, clip corners and turn the right sides out, making sure you poke the corners out to sharp points.

11. Press to neaten but be careful not to distort the felt – use a pillowcase or tea towel placed on top of the pages as you press. Fold in and press the open side seam. Insert the raw end of the tab closure into the opening and align it with the loop fastening on the front page. Leave 6–7cm of the tab hanging out of the seam and pin the gap closed.

continued on the next page

12. To add extra stability and to close up the seam opening you will need to topstitch around all edges. Stitch 0.5cm in from the edge, catching the open seam with tab closure shut to finish.

ASSEMBLE AND APPLIQUÉ THE INSIDE PAGES

13. Assemble and sew the appliqué graphics onto the front of the fabric rectangles for the inside pages just as you did for the cover and inside cover pages. Remember to leave 2cm around the edges to allow for the seam allowance and topstitching. Use the photos on pages 118, 121 and 122 as a guide as a guide as to placement.

14. Once all the appliqué has been sewn, you can stitch the pages together. Align the fabric rectangles with right sides facing and align the wadding behind them against the wrong side of the adjacent fabric. Pin and then stitch the three layers together, sewing around all edges using a 1cm seam allowance and leaving a 6cm gap for turning. Trim off any loose threads, clip the the corners and turn the right sides out. Press to neaten, folding in the open seam. Topstitch around all sides 0.5cm around the edges, catching the open seam closed as you sew. Repeat for the second pair of rectangles.

ASSEMBLE PAGES AND STITCH THE SPINE

15. Now that you have all three rectangles that will make up the cover and pages of your book sewn and topstitched, it's time to assemble the book. Place the two smaller rectangles on top of each other with all sides aligned, using the diagram below as a guide. Position these on top of the slightly larger rectangle, with the inside cover pages facing you, and centre all pages neatly, pinning into place down the mid-centre.

16. To create the book spine, stitch two parallel vertical lines approx. 2cm apart down the centre of the rectangles. Fold the book in half and bring the tab closure from the back to affix at the front to finish!

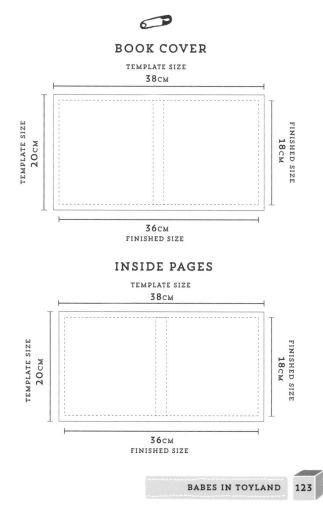

BOOK COVER

TEMPLATE SIZE 38CM

TEMPLATE SIZE 20CM

FINISHED SIZE 18CM

36CM FINISHED SIZE

INSIDE PAGES

TEMPLATE SIZE 38CM

TEMPLATE SIZE 20CM

FINISHED SIZE 18CM

36CM FINISHED SIZE

BUILDING BLOCKS

My daughter loves to build, stack and play with these handmade high-contrast blocks. The perfect playtime toy for any growing baby, blocks help build co-ordination as babies learn to grasp and hold objects. They also help to develop creative skills. Pick out a selection of bright high-contrast cotton patterns and prints to design your own 3D building blocks and fill them either with polyester toy stuffing or, if you're feeling fancy, get some foam cut to size from your local foam cutters or builder's merchant – both are soft and safe. Pair up these blocks with the colourful Patchwork Playmat on pages 132–137 for the ultimate baby playtime gift set!

HOW TO CUT THE FABRIC

1. Photocopy or trace the number templates on page 155 onto paper or thin card. Cut out the templates with paper scissors.

2. Using the square template, cut out 30 squares, which is enough to cover all five cubes. Each cube will need six squares. Cut them out in a variety of colours and patterns to create an eye-catching and mesmerising mix.

3. Use the number templates to cut out felt numbers 1–5. Decide which five fabric squares will be the front of each block, and stitch a felt number onto the right side of each square block, using either a zigzag or straight stitch if using a sewing machine or a blanket or whipstitch if sewing by hand. Make sure you sew the appliqué securely to ensure it is baby safe.

continued on the next page

FINISHED SIZE
10cm blocks (make 5)
Suitable from birth

MATERIALS
Templates (see page 155)
5 x 10cm foam cubes or enough
   polyester toy stuffing to fill
   5 x 10cm square blocks.
Assorted cotton fabrics, enough
   to give 30 x 12cm squares
Felt scraps for appliqué
Matching threads

SUPPLIES
Paper or card for templates
Paper scissors
Tape measure
Fabric marker pen or tailor's chalk
Fabric scissors
Sewing machine and/or
   hand-sewing needle
Pins

STITCHES USED
Straight stitch
Zigzag stitch (optional)
Whipstitch
Slipstitch

TEMPLATES – see page 155
Numbers

CONSTRUCT AND SEW THE SQUARES

4. Use the layout diagram opposite to see how your squares will connect to create the 3D cube shape, and lay out the squares for each of your blocks accordingly. Follow the numbers for order of construction.

5. Start off by pinning square 1 to square 2 with right sides together and all edges aligned. The corner seams of all the squares will need to intersect in order to form the 3D shape, so to ensure you get perfectly sharp corners you will need to start and stop stitching 1cm in from all corners on all sides of the squares.

6. Place the needle into the fabric 1cm in from the corner and sew a straight stitch (using a 1cm seam allowance) down one edge of the square, then stop stitching again 1cm in from the edge. Backstitch at each end to secure and trim off any loose threads.

7. Now align square 3 to square 2 with right sides together, align, pin and sew one edge together as in step 6, starting and stopping the stitching 1cm in from the edge at either side. Continue attaching and sewing the squares together in this way, following the layout diagram, until the pieces make a cube formation. Leave one seam open for stuffing.

8. Clip corners, then turn the right sides out. Stuff the foam block into the fabric cube through the open seam, moulding it into place and shifting it about until it sits nice and snug within its fabric covering. If using polyester filling, stuff the blocks until you get the desired firmness.

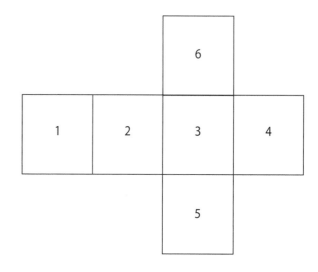

9. To finish, you will need to close up the open seam. Fold and tuck a 1cm seam allowance under and stitch closed with matching thread and a neat slipstitch.

10. Repeat steps 5–9 with the remaining squares to complete your set of baby building blocks. Now stack 'em high and get set to play!

GUITAR SOFTIE

Shake rattle and roll with this oh-so-adorable guitar softie made from a mix of bright cottons and felt appliqué. One of my favourite go-to baby gifts, this soft rock plaything can also double up as a nursery cushion or a DIY decoration. Add a rattle insert and let your baby rock on!

HOW TO

1. Photocopy or trace the guitar and guitar appliqué templates on page 149, enlarging by the percentage required, onto paper or thin card. Cut out the templates with paper scissors.

2. Pin the guitar template onto the cotton fabric and mark out the shape. Unpin, then flip the template over, pin to the fabric and mark out a second mirror-image shape. Cut out both guitar shapes.

3. Using the guitar appliqué templates, pin and mark all the details on contrasting felt scraps, using the photo on page 131 as a guide as to colours. Cut out all the shapes.

4. Build up the design of the guitar by positioning the felt pieces onto the centre of the right side of the guitar front and pin in place. Figure out the order of sewing before you start stitching as some details overlap – again, use the photo on page 131 as a guide. Sew on the appliqué details using matching threads and a small zigzag stitch if sewing on the machine or a small, neat blanket or whipstitch if sewing by hand.

continued on the next page

SIZE
50cm high

MATERIALS
Templates (see page 149)
0.5m cotton fabric
Approx 0.5m in total of assorted coloured felt for appliqué
Matching threads
Polyester toy stuffing to fill
Rattle insert (optional)

SUPPLIES
Paper or card for templates
Paper scissors
Fabric marker pen or tailor's chalk
Fabric scissors
Sewing machine and/or hand-sewing needle
Pins
Iron

STITCHES USED
Straight stitch
Zigzag stitch
Whipstitch

TEMPLATES – see page 149
Guitar and guitar appliqué details

5. Sew the tuning peg pieces together in pairs, joining around the edges with a zigzag stitch and leaving the bottom edge open. Tack the open bottom seams of the tuning peg pieces into place at the top of the guitar head with the bottom seams of the cut-outs laying flush against the outside edge so that they are facing inwards on top of the front right side of the guitar.

6. Place the guitar back piece on top of the front with all sides aligned and right sides of the fabric facing. Pin into place. The tuning pegs should be sandwiched in between the front and back pieces.

7. Stitch the two guitar pieces together using a straight stitch and a 1cm seam allowance, leaving a 6cm gap along one of the straight edges for turning.

8. Trim, clip, snip and notch the seam allowance to prevent extra bulkiness. Turn the right sides out making sure to press all the angles and points into shape.

9. Stuff the guitar with polyester toy stuffing until you get the preferred firmness, adding the rattle insert as you go, if you are using one. Stitch the open seam closed with some matching thread and a neat whipstitch.

PATCHWORK PLAYMAT

A bright and colourful playmat makes a unique style statement for any modern baby's nursery, plus is perfect for stimulating their senses and developing eyesight as they explore high-contrast patterns and bright colours. This playmat is made up from an oversized patchwork block using the half-square triangle technique similar to the Chevron Baby Quilt on pages 26–31. A half-square triangle is simply a square block made up from two triangles. The quilt is both easy to fold up and store away as well as cushioned and comfy – perfect for tummy time to encourage babies to roll around, sit up and explore toys. Pair it with the Building Blocks on pages 124–127 for the ultimate baby gift.

HOW TO CUT THE FABRIC

1. Draw a playmat square block template measuring 20 x 20cm onto paper or thin card. Cut out the template with paper scissors.

2. Using the template, mark and cut out the required number of squares from all six fabrics as indicated in the materials list opposite.

3. Prepare all the squares for sewing by sorting them into eight pairs, using the photo opposite and the instructions below as your guide:

    🏀 2 pairs A and B for 4 half-square triangles

    🏀 2 pairs C and F for 4 half-square triangles

    🏀 1 pair C and D for 2 half-square triangles

    🏀 1 pair C and E for 2 half-square triangles

    🏀 1 pair D and F for 2 half-square triangles

    🏀 1 pair E and F for 2 half-square triangles

continued on the next page

FINISHED SIZE
82 x 82cm

MATERIALS
Selection of quilting cotton fabrics in 6 different colours:

🏀 0.25m colour A; 2 squares

🏀 0.25m colour B; 2 squares

🏀 0.5m colour C; 4 squares

🏀 0.25m colour D; 2 squares

🏀 0.25m colour E; 2 squares

🏀 0.5m colour F; 4 squares

1.5m cotton fabric for backing and border strips

Matching threads

1m wadding

SUPPLIES
Paper or card for template

Paper scissors

Fabric marker pen or tailor's chalk

Rotary cutter, mat and ruler or fabric scissors

Pins

Sewing machine and/or hand-sewing needle

Iron

STITCHES USED
Straight stitch

SEW THE HALF-SQUARE TRIANGLES

4. To create a half-square triangle, pin two fabric squares together with right sides facing, then use a ruler and a fabric pen to mark out a diagonal line from top left corner to bottom right corner onto the wrong side of the fabric facing upwards. Next, sew a straight seam exactly 6mm above the diagonal line, and another one exactly 6mm below the diagonal line. Then cut along the diagonal line to reveal two half-square triangles.

5. Repeat step 4 for the remaining seven pairs of squares, so you have 16 half-square triangle blocks in total.

6. Press the half-square triangle blocks on the back with the seams towards the darker fabric, then lightly press again on the front of each fabric square for a neat finish. Trim off all the little overhanging corner seams to create 16 perfect squares.

ASSEMBLE, JOIN AND SEW THE PATCHWORK

7. Lay the blocks on a flat surface in four rows of four, using the layout diagram opposite as a guide as to placement.

8. The blocks will be sewn together in rows first. Begin the stitching with the top row. Pin the square blocks together with all edges aligned and right sides of the fabric facing, then sew together using a straight stitch and an exact 6mm seam allowance. Be careful to match up the corner seams as neatly as possible as this

will help keep your pattern accurate and exact. Press the joining seams open. Repeat for the next three rows until you have four strips of four blocks.

9. Once all the rows have been sewn and pressed, you can start joining them together to build up the pattern. Refer to the layout diagram opposite as you pin and stitch the rows together with the right sides of the fabric facing, again using an exact 6mm seam allowance. Be sure to match up the seams as you sew to ensure a perfect pattern.

10. Press the seams open at the back of the patchwork, then press the front of the playmat top to neaten. Finally, square up the patchwork, trimming the edges a little if necessary, so you have a 72cm square.

MAKE THE BORDERS

11. Your finished patchwork block should now measure 72 x 72cm and will need a border to frame it for a fancy finish. Cut out four strips from the backing fabric measuring 82 x 6cm to create a fabric border for each edge of the patchwork playmat. (As you will need to mitre the corners of the border strips the fabric must be cut a little longer than the finished patchwork sides.)

continued on the next page

FINAL DIMENSIONS & COLOUR LAYOUT GUIDE

82CM x 82CM

5CM
BORDER

16 SQUARES / 32 TRIANGLES

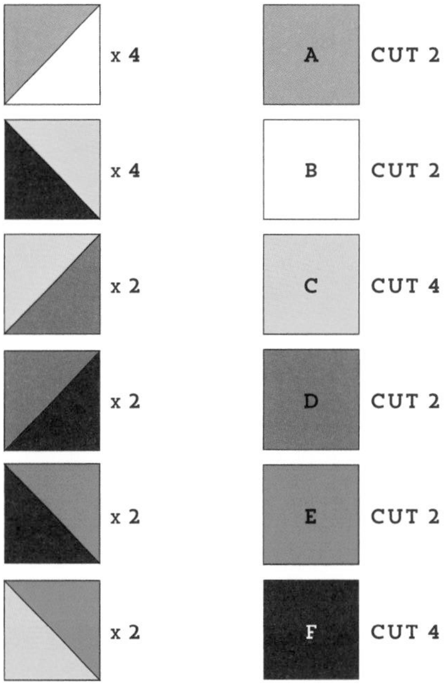

x 4

x 4

x 2

x 2

x 2

x 2

A   CUT 2

B   CUT 2

C   CUT 4

D   CUT 2

E   CUT 2

F   CUT 4

12. Find the middle of both the lengthwise border edges and the patchwork sides by folding them in half. Place pins at the centre points as markers. Unfold and line up the centre points of all the edges and pin the border strips to the patchwork with right sides of the fabric facing.

13. Join the border strips to all edges of the patchwork using a straight stitch and 0.5cm seam allowance, and starting/stopping stitching 0.5cm in from the edges of the patchwork and backstitch at each end to make sure the stitching is secure. Press the seam allowance towards the border.

14. To join the corners together you will need to mitre them. Mitred corners come together at a 45-degree angle to form an angled seam. Fold the patchwork in half along the diagonal with right sides of the fabric together to form a triangle. Line up the borders strips so that they are sitting on top of each other.

15. Take a ruler and a fabric marker – use the ruler to follow the line of the folded patchwork edge across and towards the furthest corner of the border strips and mark the line. Pin the border strips into position and stitch along the marked line, beginning the seam from the last stitch you made along the border seam line to ensure no gaps will appear from the front. Backstitch at both the beginning and the end and trim off the extra fabric along the angled seam approx. 6mm from the edge. Repeat for the remaining three corners and press the seams open.

ASSEMBLE AND FINISH THE PLAYMAT

16. Now you have completed the patchwork top and added the borders it's time to finish the playmat by adding the wadding and the backing. Cut the wadding and the backing to the same size as the patchwork top. Make sure the backing is pressed and neat.

17. Assemble the three layers by laying the patchwork top against the backing fabric with right sides facing together and all edges aligned. Position the wadding behind the backing so that the patchwork top and the backing are sitting on top of the wadding and pin all three layers together.

18. Stitch the layers together by sewing around all sides using a straight stitch and a 0.5cm seam allowance. Leave a 6cm gap for turning along one edge.

19. Clip the corners and turn the right sides out. Press to neaten. Hand-sew the open seam closed with a neat whipstitch and some matching thread.

20. Finally, topstitch along the seam line of the borders to join all three layers together. To further prevent the patchwork playmat from loosing its shape once washed, secure the layers together by adding some additional topstitching along the seam lines of the patchwork pattern.

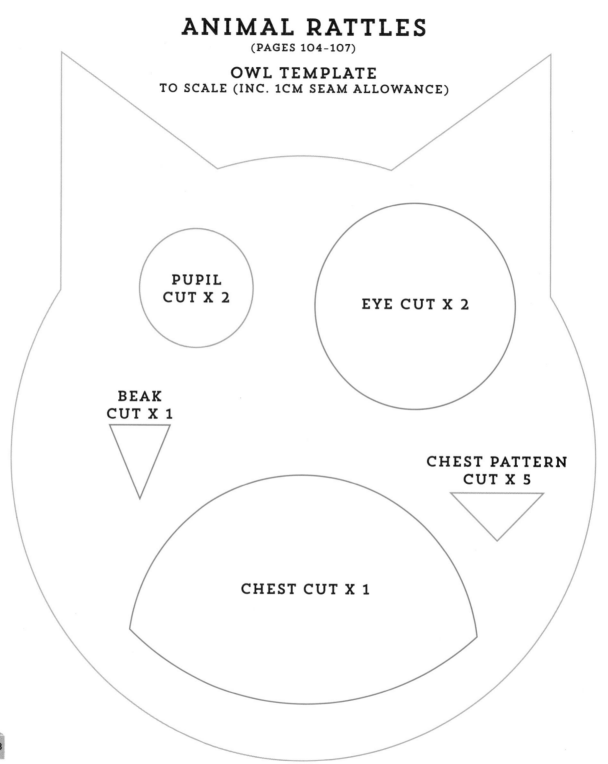

ANIMAL RATTLES
(PAGES 104-107)

OWL TEMPLATE
TO SCALE (INC. 1CM SEAM ALLOWANCE)

PUPIL
CUT X 2

EYE CUT X 2

BEAK
CUT X 1

CHEST PATTERN
CUT X 5

CHEST CUT X 1

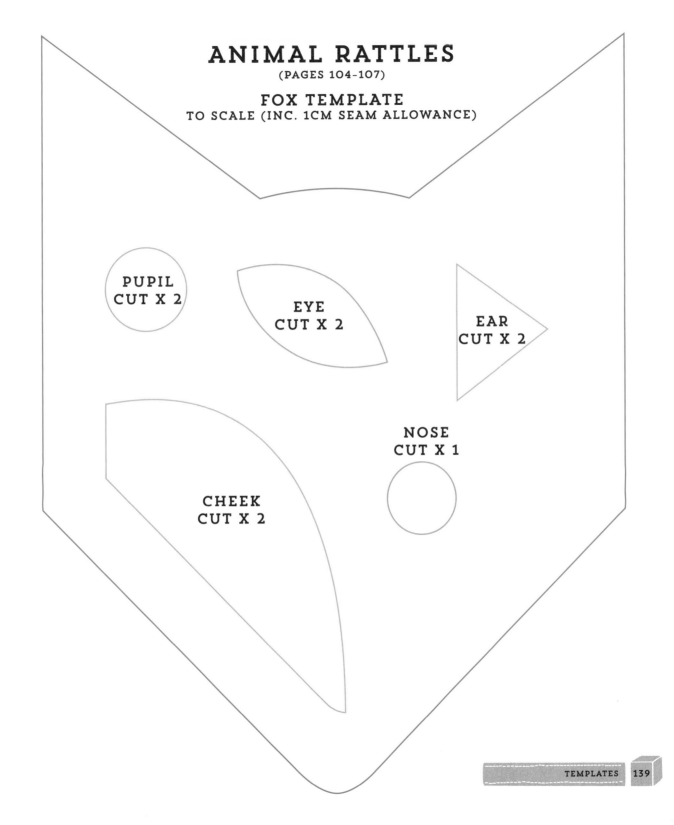

ANIMAL RATTLES

(PAGES 104–107)

FOX TEMPLATE
TO SCALE (INC. 1CM SEAM ALLOWANCE)

PUPIL
CUT X 2

EYE
CUT X 2

EAR
CUT X 2

NOSE
CUT X 1

CHEEK
CUT X 2

ANIMAL RATTLES

(PAGES 104–107)

PANDA TEMPLATE
TO SCALE (INC. 1CM SEAM ALLOWANCE)

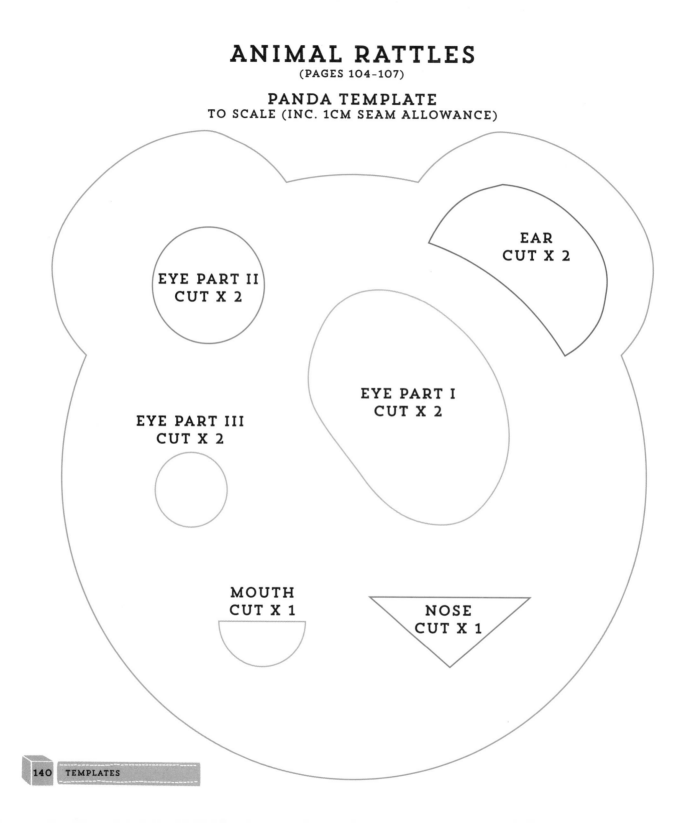

EAR
CUT X 2

EYE PART II
CUT X 2

EYE PART I
CUT X 2

EYE PART III
CUT X 2

MOUTH
CUT X 1

NOSE
CUT X 1

APPLIQUÉ ONESIES

(PAGES 40-43)

TO SCALE

REVERSIBLE BABY BONNET

(PAGES 74–77)

TEMPLATES
SCALE UP 200%

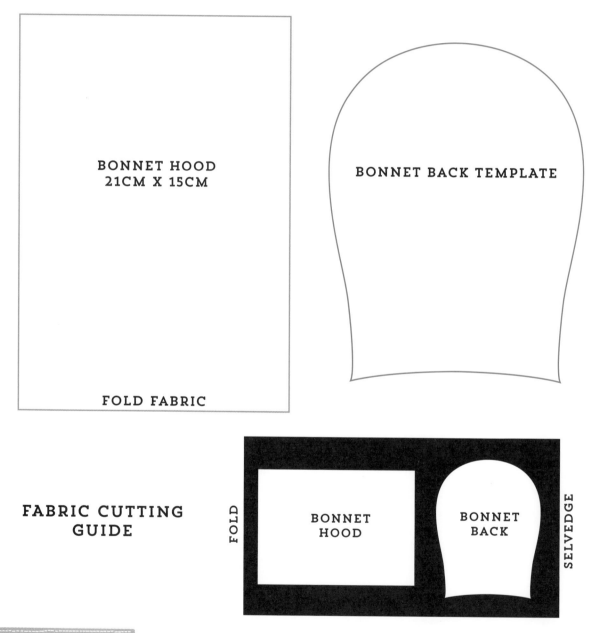

BONNET HOOD
21CM X 15CM

FOLD FABRIC

BONNET BACK TEMPLATE

FABRIC CUTTING GUIDE

FOLD

BONNET
HOOD

BONNET
BACK

SELVEDGE

BABY GARLAND

(PAGES 110–113)

SHAPES CUT X 1
BACKINGS CUT X 2

SCALE UP 150%

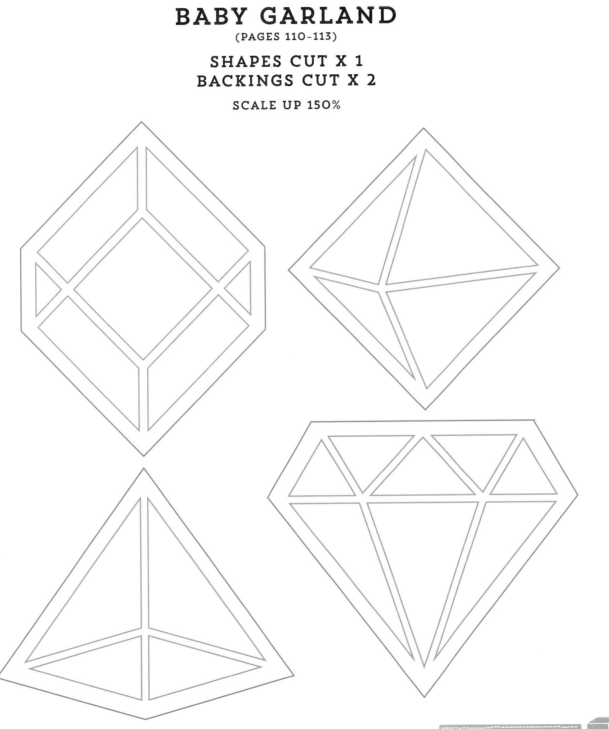

FELT MOCCASINS

(PAGES 78–83)

TO SCALE

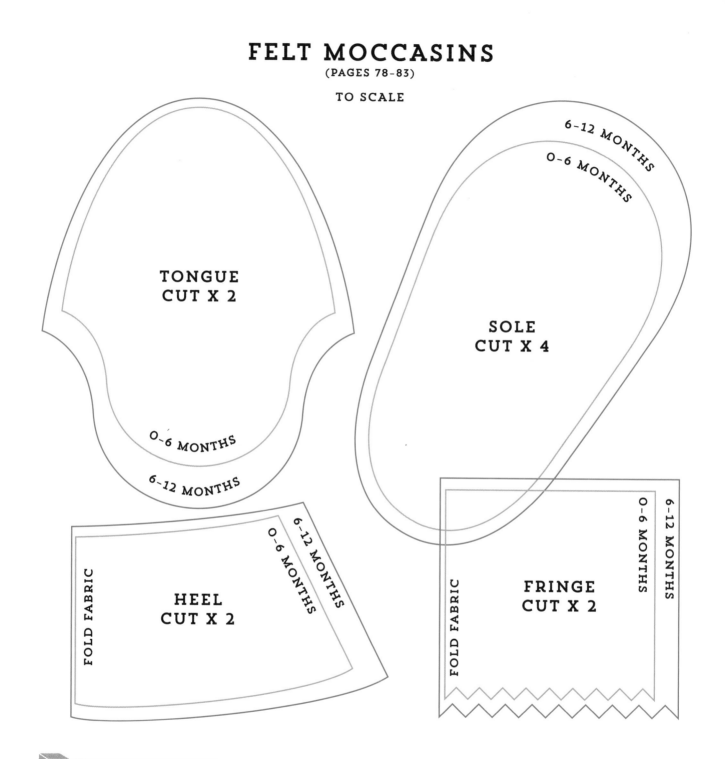

TONGUE
CUT X 2

0–6 MONTHS

6–12 MONTHS

6–12 MONTHS

0–6 MONTHS

SOLE
CUT X 4

HEEL
CUT X 2

FOLD FABRIC

6–12 MONTHS

0–6 MONTHS

FRINGE
CUT X 2

FOLD FABRIC

0–6 MONTHS

6–12 MONTHS

CHEVRON BABY QUILT

(PAGES 26-31)

FULL SIZE LAYOUT
TOTAL 54 SQUARES/108 TRIANGLES

60CM
6 SQUARES
12 TRIANGLES

90CM – 9 SQUARES/18 TRIANGLES

SQUARE/TRIANGLE
TEMPLATE

SCALE UP 200%

BABY'S BEST BLOOMERS

(PAGES 86-91)

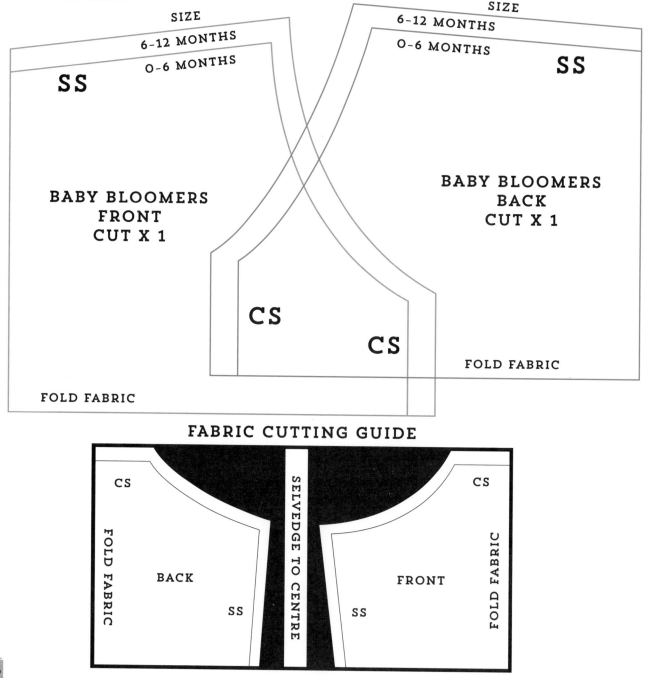

SCALE UP 200%

SIZE
6-12 MONTHS
0-6 MONTHS

SS

BABY BLOOMERS
FRONT
CUT X 1

SIZE
6-12 MONTHS
0-6 MONTHS

SS

BABY BLOOMERS
BACK
CUT X 1

CS

CS

FOLD FABRIC

FOLD FABRIC

FABRIC CUTTING GUIDE

CS

CS

FOLD FABRIC

BACK

SS

SELVEDGE TO CENTRE

FRONT

SS

FOLD FABRIC

RAINCLOUD & THUNDERCLOUD MOBILES

(PAGES 36–39)

DIMENSIONS

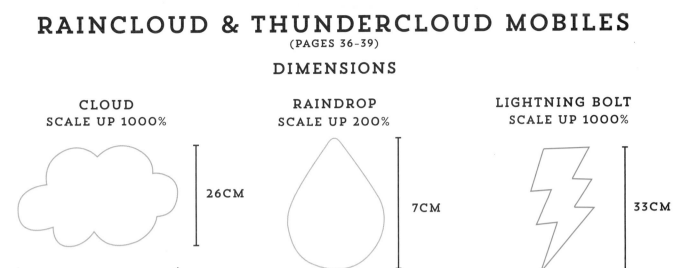

CLOUD
SCALE UP 1000%

26CM

44CM

RAINDROP
SCALE UP 200%

7CM

5.34CM

LIGHTNING BOLT
SCALE UP 1000%

33CM

APPROX. 18.5CM

BABY BANDANA BIBS

(PAGES 72–73)

SCALE UP 200%

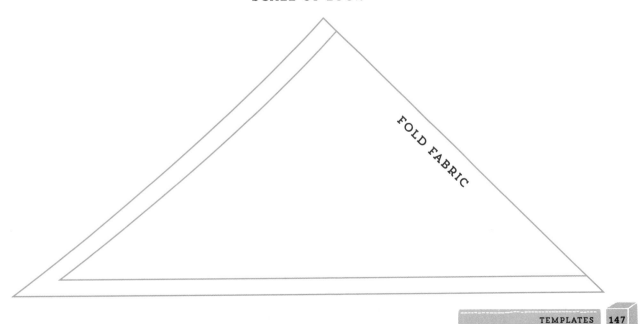

FOLD FABRIC

BLANKEY BUDDY

(PAGES 54–59)

PANDA HEAD TEMPLATE
TO SCALE

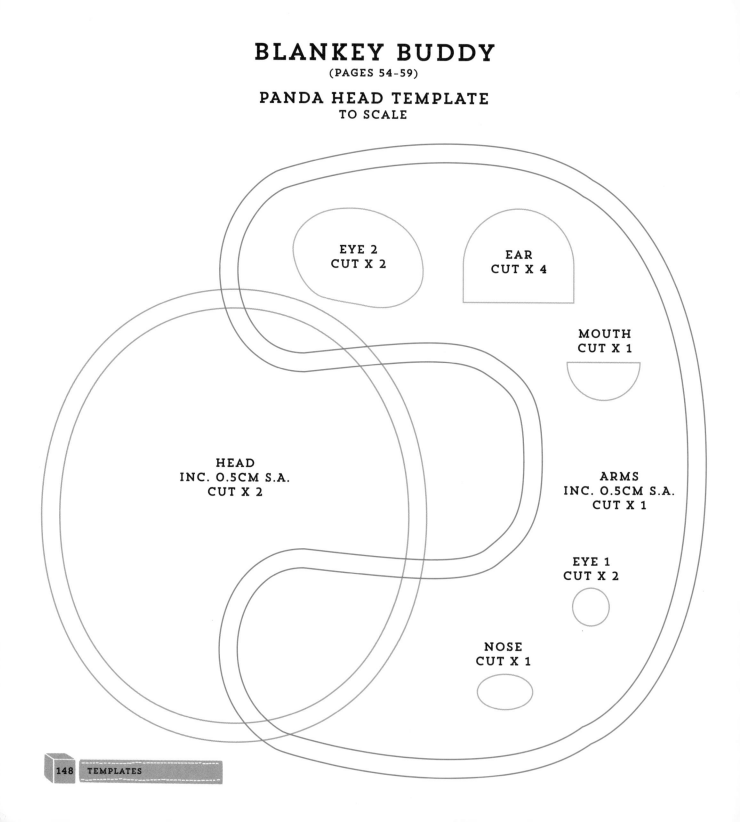

EYE 2
CUT X 2

EAR
CUT X 4

MOUTH
CUT X 1

HEAD
INC. 0.5CM S.A.
CUT X 2

ARMS
INC. 0.5CM S.A.
CUT X 1

EYE 1
CUT X 2

NOSE
CUT X 1

GUITAR SOFTIE

(PAGES 128–131)

TO SCALE

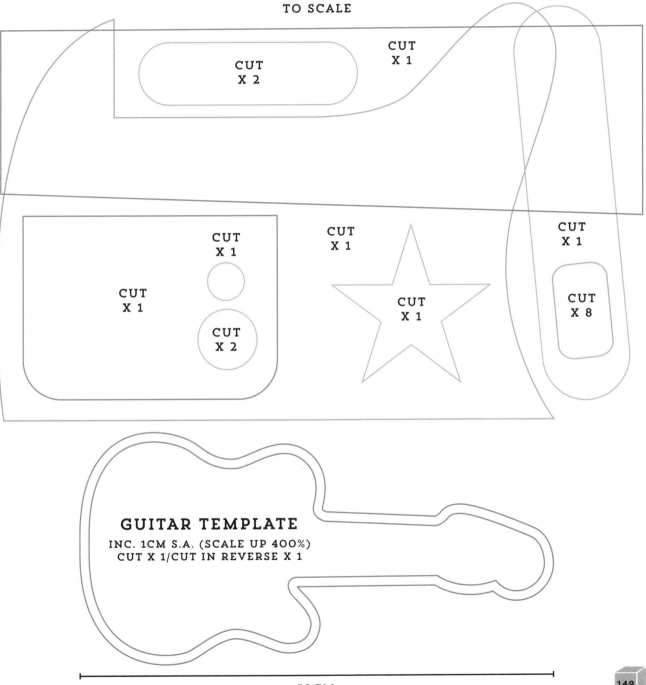

CUT
X 2

CUT
X 1

CUT
X 1

CUT
X 1

CUT
X 1

CUT
X 1

CUT
X 8

CUT
X 1

CUT
X 1

CUT
X 2

CUT
X 1

GUITAR TEMPLATE

INC. 1CM S.A. (SCALE UP 400%)
CUT X 1/CUT IN REVERSE X 1

52CM

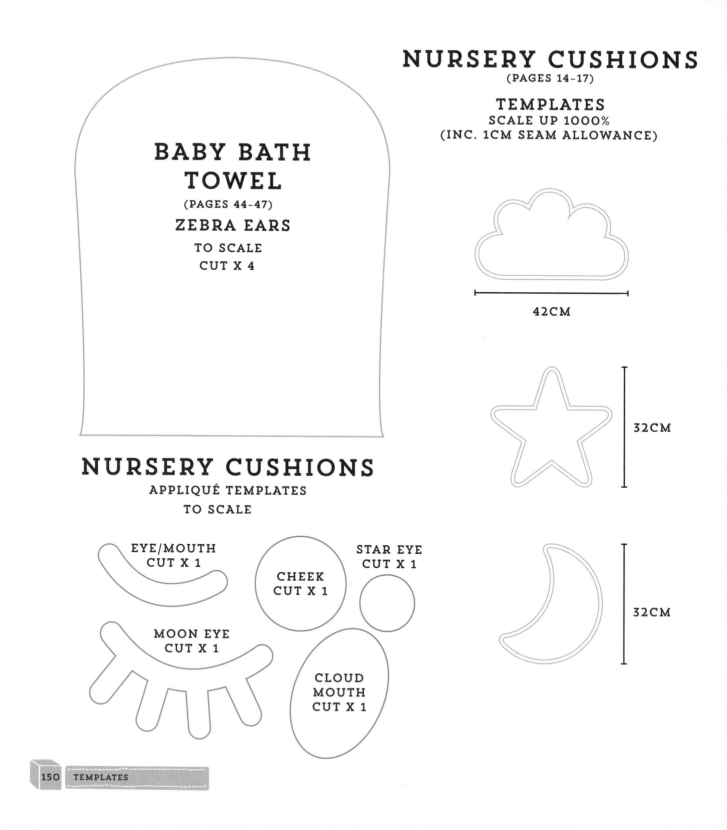

BABY BATH TOWEL

(PAGES 44–47)

ZEBRA EARS

TO SCALE
CUT X 4

NURSERY CUSHIONS

(PAGES 14–17)

TEMPLATES

SCALE UP 1000%
(INC. 1CM SEAM ALLOWANCE)

42CM

32CM

32CM

NURSERY CUSHIONS

APPLIQUÉ TEMPLATES
TO SCALE

EYE/MOUTH
CUT X 1

CHEEK
CUT X 1

STAR EYE
CUT X 1

MOON EYE
CUT X 1

CLOUD
MOUTH
CUT X 1

DIY PRAM TOY

(PAGES 60-63)

APPLIQUÉ TEMPLATES
SCALE UP 150%

EYE DETAIL
CUT X 1

EYE DETAIL
CUT X 1

WING DETAIL 2
CUT X 2

TAIL DETAIL 3
CUT X 3

TAIL DETAIL 2
CUT X 1

CHEST DETAIL
CUT X 3

WING DETAIL 1
CUT X 6

TAIL DETAIL 1
CUT X 2

BEAK
0.5CM S.A.
CUT X 2

WING DETAIL 2
CUT X 2

PRAM TOY TEMPLATE
INC. 0.5CM S.A. (SCALE UP 150%)

FOLD FABRIC

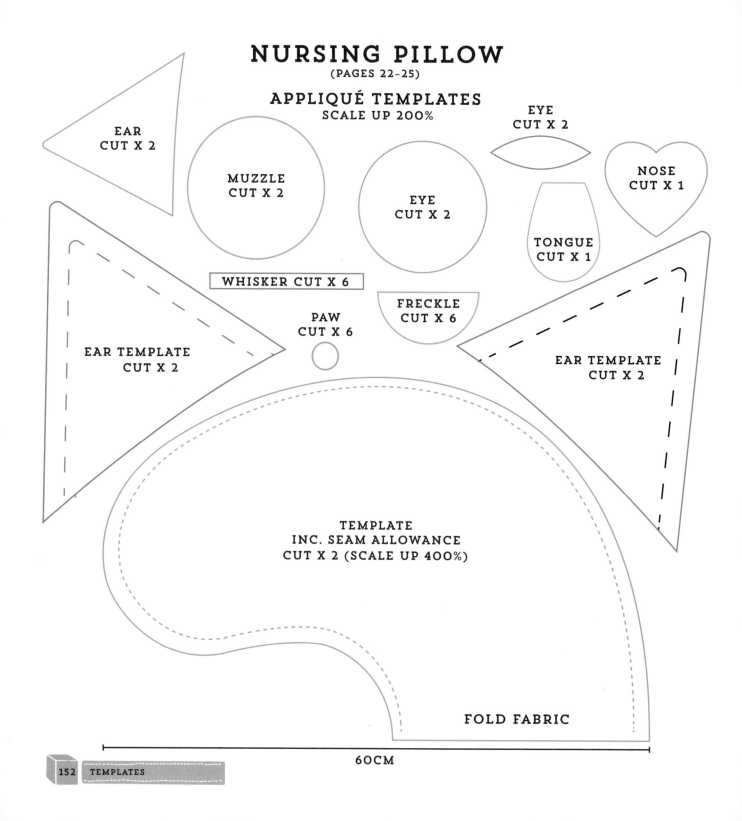

NURSING PILLOW

(PAGES 22–25)

APPLIQUÉ TEMPLATES
SCALE UP 200%

EAR
CUT X 2

MUZZLE
CUT X 2

EYE
CUT X 2

EYE
CUT X 2

NOSE
CUT X 1

TONGUE
CUT X 1

WHISKER CUT X 6

EAR TEMPLATE
CUT X 2

PAW
CUT X 6

FRECKLE
CUT X 6

EAR TEMPLATE
CUT X 2

TEMPLATE
INC. SEAM ALLOWANCE
CUT X 2 (SCALE UP 400%)

FOLD FABRIC

60CM

BABY BOOK

(PAGES 118–123)

GRAPHICS TEMPLATES
SCALE UP 200%

BABY'S FIRST FLASH CARDS

SHAPES TEMPLATES
TO SCALE

BABY'S FIRST FLASH CARDS

(PAGES 108–109)

NUMBER TEMPLATES
TO SCALE

*THE 6 CAN ALSO BE THE 9

SOFT STACKING RINGS

(PAGES 114–117)

ALL TEMPLATES INCLUDE SEAM ALLOWANCE
SCALE UP 200%

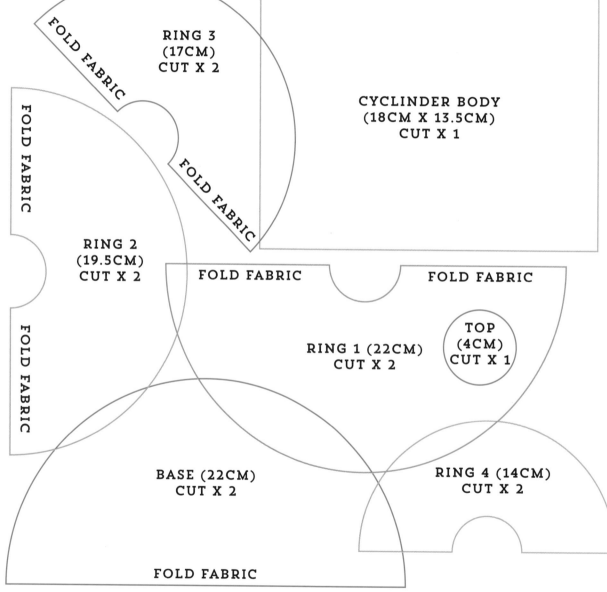

FOLD FABRIC

RING 3
(17CM)
CUT X 2

FOLD FABRIC

CYCLINDER BODY
(18CM X 13.5CM)
CUT X 1

FOLD FABRIC

FOLD FABRIC

RING 2
(19.5CM)
CUT X 2

FOLD FABRIC

FOLD FABRIC

RING 1 (22CM)
CUT X 2

TOP
(4CM)
CUT X 1

BASE (22CM)
CUT X 2

RING 4 (14CM)
CUT X 2

FOLD FABRIC

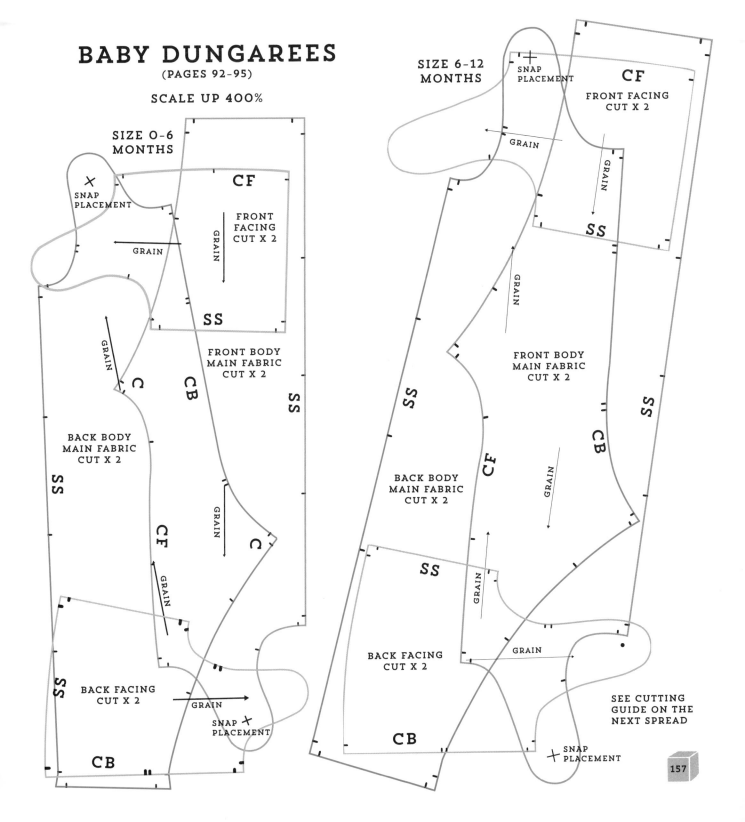

BABY DUNGAREES

(PAGES 92-95)

SCALE UP 400%

SIZE 0-6
MONTHS

SNAP
PLACEMENT

CF

FRONT
FACING
CUT X 2

GRAIN

GRAIN

SS

FRONT BODY
MAIN FABRIC
CUT X 2

GRAIN

CB

SS

BACK BODY
MAIN FABRIC
CUT X 2

SS

CF

GRAIN

CF

GRAIN

SS

BACK FACING
CUT X 2

GRAIN

SNAP
PLACEMENT

CB

SIZE 6-12
MONTHS

SNAP
PLACEMENT

CF

FRONT FACING
CUT X 2

GRAIN

GRAIN

SS

GRAIN

FRONT BODY
MAIN FABRIC
CUT X 2

SS

SS

CF

CB

BACK BODY
MAIN FABRIC
CUT X 2

GRAIN

GRAIN

SS

GRAIN

BACK FACING
CUT X 2

GRAIN

SEE CUTTING
GUIDE ON THE
NEXT SPREAD

CB

SNAP
PLACEMENT

157

BABY SLUMBER SACK

(PAGES 32–35)

SCALE UP 400%

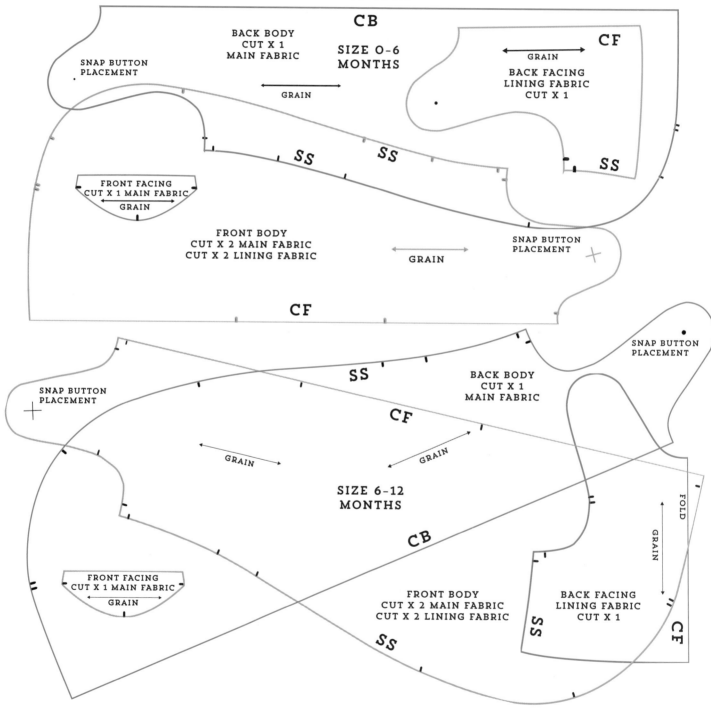

CB

BACK BODY
CUT X 1
MAIN FABRIC

SIZE 0–6
MONTHS

CF

GRAIN

BACK FACING
LINING FABRIC
CUT X 1

SNAP BUTTON
PLACEMENT

GRAIN

SS

SS

SS

FRONT FACING
CUT X 1 MAIN FABRIC

GRAIN

FRONT BODY
CUT X 2 MAIN FABRIC
CUT X 2 LINING FABRIC

GRAIN

SNAP BUTTON
PLACEMENT

CF

SS

SNAP BUTTON
PLACEMENT

BACK BODY
CUT X 1
MAIN FABRIC

SNAP BUTTON
PLACEMENT

CF

GRAIN

GRAIN

SIZE 6–12
MONTHS

FOLD

GRAIN

CB

FRONT FACING
CUT X 1 MAIN FABRIC

GRAIN

FRONT BODY
CUT X 2 MAIN FABRIC
CUT X 2 LINING FABRIC

BACK FACING
LINING FABRIC
CUT X 1

SS

CF

SS

FABRIC CUTTING GUIDES

NOT TO SCALE

BABY DUNGAREES
(PAGES 92-95)

FOLD

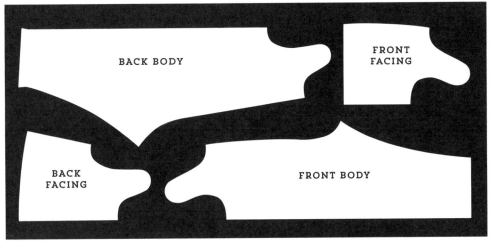

BACK BODY

FRONT FACING

BACK FACING

FRONT BODY

SELVEDGE

BABY SLUMBER SACK
(PAGES 32-35)

FOLD

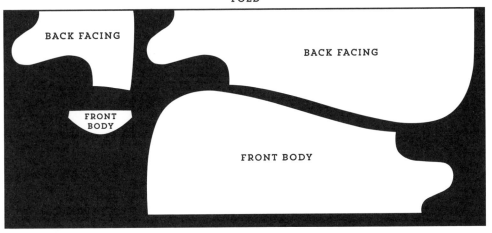

BACK FACING

BACK FACING

FRONT BODY

FRONT BODY

SELVEDGE

ACKNOWLEDGEMENTS

I would like to thank the following suppliers for providing clothes and equipment to be used for the photography in the book:

OLIVE LOVES ALFIE
www.olivelovesalfie.co.uk

BORN
www.kidsen.co.uk

KIDSEN
www.kidsen.co.uk

SCP
www.scp.co.uk

NUBIE
www.nubie.co.uk

SMUG
www.ifeelsmug.com

POLARN O.PYRET
www.polarnopyret.co.uk

OH BABY LONDON
www.ohbabylondon.com

GENTLY ELEPHANT
www.gentlyelephant.co.uk

I would also like to personally acknowledge all those who helped me make this book happen!

Thanks to Rowan Lawton, my agent and to the whole team at Kyle Books, especially to Vicky Orchard my editor and to the rest of #TeamSewTiny including Polly Webb-Wilson for super-styling, Laura Edwards for capturing it all with her fabulous photography and to Anita Mangan for bringing it all together with her design and illustrative touches.

Thanks and love also to all my friends and family for putting up with me and supporting me in the process of writing and sewing and of course to Brian, my constant collaborator, whose design skills and creative input I would be lost without.

And lastly to my little one, Boudica Venus May, my mini muse who inspired it all in the first place!

www.jazzdominoholly.co.uk

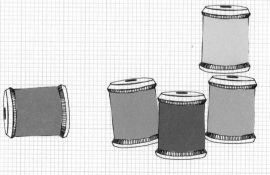